THE NEW
BRAZIL

THE NEW BRAZIL

Riordan Roett

BROOKINGS INSTITUTION PRESS
Washington, D.C.

Copyright © 2010
THE BROOKINGS INSTITUTION
1775 Massachusetts Avenue, N.W., Washington, D.C. 20036
www.brookings.edu

Library of Congress Cataloging-in-Publication data
Roett, Riordan, 1938–
  The new Brazil / Riordan Roett.
    p.   cm.
  Includes bibliographical references and index.
  Summary: "Recounts Brazil's evolution from remote Portuguese colony, through economic crises that led to more prudent monetary policies, and to its new status as a regional leader, a respected ambassador for the developing world, and an increasingly important partner for the United States and European Union"—Provided by publisher.
  ISBN 978-0-8157-0423-2 (hardcover : alk. paper)
  1. Brazil—Economic conditions—1985– 2. Brazil—Economic policy—2003–
3. Brazil—Foreign economic relations. 4. Brazil—Foreign relations—1985– I. Title.
  HC187.R6438 2010
  330.981—dc22   2010019409

9 8 7 6 5 4 3 2 1

Printed on acid-free paper

Typeset in Sabon and Strayhorn

Composition by Circle Graphics
Columbia, Maryland

Printed by R. R. Donnelley
Harrisonburg, Virginia

Contents

Acknowledgments

I would like to thank the individuals who played a role in the completion of this volume. For their research and project assistance, I am indebted to Lauren A. F. Miller, Kevin Hempel, Alexandre C. Borges, and Benjamin Rinaker. For general editing and project management support, I would like to thank Guadalupe Paz. For their invaluable feedback, I owe special thanks to the anonymous reviewers of the preliminary manuscript.

Finally, I would like to recognize several individuals at the Brookings Institution Press who were instrumental in making this project a reality: Christopher J. Kelaher, marketing director and senior acquisitions editor; Mary Kwak, acquisitions editor, for her detailed comments and suggestions; Larry Converse, production manager, in charge of typesetting and printing; Susan Woollen, art coordinator, responsible for the cover design; and Janet Walker, managing editor.

To all other individuals who directly or indirectly played a role in the production of this book, I would also like to express my gratitude.

THE NEW
BRAZIL

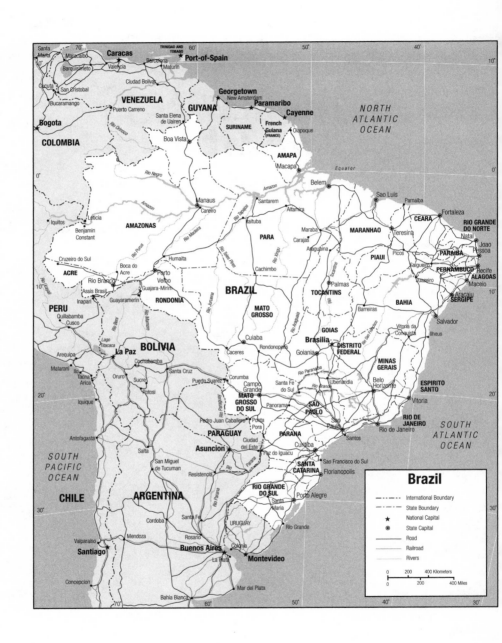

Brazil

-·-·-·-·-	International Boundary	
-·-·-·-·-	State Boundary	
★	National Capital	
⊛	State Capital	
——	Road	
——	Railroad	
——	Rivers	

0	200	400 Kilometers
0	200	400 Miles

1

Introduction: The New Brazil

An unpredictable process of economic and social reform that began with the election of Fernando Henrique Cardoso in 1994 will reach a plateau in 2010 with the successful conclusion of the presidency of Luiz Inácio (Lula) da Silva. Both presidencies deserve credit for taking the difficult decision to modernize the country and create the conditions for the emergence of the new Brazil. After the return to democracy in 1985, Brazil lost a decade with three mediocre, if well-meaning, presidents before Cardoso and a new team of economists were able to restart the economy and provide the framework for stable growth, social reform, and institutional stability.

The modernization process in Brazil has not been seamless. Mistakes have been made. Politics often have slowed the process of change, and indeed, as this book illustrates, while there has been real progress in the social and economic arenas, the political system is a long way from being classified as transparent and accountable. But, in part, the story of the new Brazil is that it has happened without—or in spite of—the "old" politics of patronage and corruption. While that too is changing slowly, a great deal of catch-up is needed in the twenty-first century.

After an introduction to the history of Brazil, which is essential to understanding what has transpired since 2004, this book analyzes the complex path to sustained growth that the country has taken. In part the success is due to external factors such as the high demand for Brazilian exports, particularly in China and the rest of Asia. But it also reflects sophisticated policy choices, including inflation targeting and maintenance of an autonomous central bank.

Brazil was one of the last of the emerging-market economies to be affected by the 2008–09 world financial and economic crisis. It was also one of the first to emerge relatively unscathed. That was as much due to careful management of the crisis by the Lula government as to the institutional reform process that began in 2004, which allowed the country to pursue countercyclical policies. It is now predicted that growth in Brazil and many of the emerging-market economies will outdistance that in the United States and the European Union in the immediate future. Brazil's GDP will probably grow more than 6 percent in 2010, compared to an average of 4.6 percent for Latin America, and it will benefit from a rebound in world commodity prices, recovering from a significant decline in late 2008.

Foreign direct investment (FDI) is also predicted to support Brazil's robust growth in 2010 and thereafter. It is estimated that Brazil will attract $35 billion in new investment in 2010, with sustained flows in the following years.[1] The national unemployment rate is heading to historic lows given the rapid recovery of the economy after the crisis and the increase in consumer demand. With rapid growth, the authorities will need to monitor inflation carefully, but the innovative program of inflation targeting, in place for some years, should obviate any serious concern about out-of-control inflation.

The international image of Brazil has been enhanced by impressive oil and natural gas discoveries off the southeast coast, which will propel the country to become an important energy exporter within six to eight years. Brazil today is not only self-sufficient in oil production, but also the second largest producer of sugar-based ethanol, a biofuel that further enhances Brazil's position as an important player in the energy field worldwide.

The pragmatic management of the largest economy in Latin America has allowed the government to target poverty—if not inequality. The first poverty reduction programs were begun under the Cardoso administration and deepened under the Lula government. After some administrative difficulties, the Bolsa Família (Family Basket) program of conditional cash transfers has resulted in tens of millions of Brazilians moving out of absolute poverty and into the consumer market and the lower middle class for the first time since the discovery of the country in 1500. Although for some the Bolsa Família program is just another set of handouts, the majority of observers believe that the conditionality and the methodology employed ensure transparency and accountability. No matter the opinion of the analysts, the program has become extraordinarily popular and probably accounted for Lula's second-term election victory in 2006, as millions of Brazilians in the underdeveloped north and northeast regions voted for Lula, in some cases against entrenched, conservative interests. Given that reality, the new government, no matter which coalition is successful in the late 2010 election, will find it difficult, if not impossible, to tamper with Bolsa Família and will probably seek to expand its scope.

The successful economic reform program that has allowed the governments of Fernando Henrique Cardoso and Lula to address long-pending social issues has helped to consolidate the national political system. Although far from perfect, the political process works in Brazil. While at times somewhat populist in nature in the post-1985 era, since the election of President Cardoso in 1994 the dynamics of the political process have been impressive. Nationwide elections are carefully monitored. Up-to-date technology precludes doubts about the outcome. There are few, if any, serious challenges to the process at any level of government—national, state, or municipal. This says little about the quality of the candidates elected, but it does emphasize the capacity of the state to manage elections peacefully in a country of 190 million inhabitants.

As the reform program advanced after 1993–94, observers noted that changes in the international system were providing space for new emerging-market actors. One acronym—BRIC—came to characterize the rise of Brazil, Russia, India, and China as new players with expanding economic potential. The BRICs have slowly gained greater influence over the international decisionmaking process, which had been dominated by the major industrial countries—the G-7—since the end of World War II. The new group of international actors has strong differences—Brazil and India are vibrant democracies, Russia is considered a soft authoritarian state, and China remains a full-fledged communist state, but with an interesting market orientation. Since the start of the twenty-first century, there have been important points of convergence on broad issues such as a new global trade regime, a new financial architecture, and an expanded role of the BRIC countries in the workings of the multilateral financial institutions in Washington, such as the International Monetary Fund (IMF) and the World Bank.

Brazil's emergence as a new player in world affairs could not have been predicted just two decades ago. The historical context is highly relevant, of course. The cold war ended in 1989. The administration of President George H. W. Bush prudently and successfully faced down an aggressive dictator in Iraq to restore a modicum of stability in the Middle East. The United States stood as the only superpower in the world. And as many analysts have pointed out, the world was on the verge of the phenomenon of globalization. Thomas Friedman, for example, stated, "Globalization is not just a trend, not just a phenomenon, not just an economic fad. It is the international system that has replaced the cold-war system."[2] Around that time, Michael Mandelbaum argued that a certain set of ideas had conquered the world in the twenty-first century: peace, democracy, and free markets.[3] The Clinton administration, which took office in January 1993, embodied this new reality. For the new Democratic White House, technology was the key to managing and dominating the new era. While reluctant to call it an "American era," U.S. policymakers clearly believed that the country "owned" globalization.[4] And if technology and knowledge were the drivers of the new era, it was clear to the White House that the United States would be the preeminent player on the field. It was widely believed that the American model had trumped all others.

The first report identifying Brazil, Russia, India, and China as the BRICs was published in 2001 by Goldman Sachs.[5] Subsequent papers refined the concept and research on the BRICs. Although the Goldman Sachs analysis did not address the geopolitical and foreign policy aspects of the post-1989 world, it gave us another side of the prism. While the United States appeared to be the unqualified "winner" from the fall of communism, the new economic order that was emerging in the 1990s had profound political, social, and cultural implications. Although in an immediate sense it was about profit (particularly for U.S. multinationals and banks), as Bacevich states, globalization was ultimately about power: "On the surface it promised a new economic order that would benefit all. Beneath the surface it implied a reconfiguring of the international political order as well."[6] This did not resonate with American political leaders who saw little, if any, obstacle to the spread of the American dream around the globe.

While there might have been other candidates for assuming the leadership of the rapidly developing economies, in coining the term BRICs, Goldman Sachs captured the imagination of analysts, investors, and ultimately journalists and policymakers. As the old order slowly evolved, the new order was not going to be as predictable as some analysts thought in the early years of the new century. This was the genius of the Goldman Sachs analysis. New players were emerging; as important, a new generation of leaders appeared in each of the four countries that embodied the shifting sands of the era. They were not, and could not be, members of the traditional G-7.[7] But they were going to gain influence and international presence for two reasons. The first was the pace of internal institutional reform; in different ways, each of the BRIC countries began to think about fiscal discipline, competitiveness, and the insertion of their economies into the international order. The second was external. An extraordinary period of economic growth and financial diversification characterized most of the years of the first decade of the new century.

Obstacles along the Road

The road to "BRIC-dom" was not without challenges. The 1990s saw the rise of the Asian Tigers, in particular the apparently inexorable rise of Japan, and much was made of a new model of economic growth and development.[8] This first phase of rapid growth collapsed in 1997 with the financial crisis that erupted in Thailand in July of that year. The contagion spread across Asia and into 1998 (bringing down Japan in the process), it hit Russia in mid-1998, and it finally ended with the collapse of the Brazilian currency in January 1999.[9] The IMF stepped in with a series of draconian conditions that drove most economies into a freefall. The crisis also opened a wide-ranging debate about the role of the multilateral institutions, their misunderstanding of the crisis, and their politically inept day-to-day handling of the situation on the ground.[10]

While Brazil was the Latin American country most affected by the 1997–98 Asian crisis, the region had its own causes for malaise. Formulated in the late 1980s and early 1990s, the so-called "Washington consensus" provided a blueprint of market-oriented reforms that should have led to increased competitiveness, greater job growth, and poverty reduction. But it did not work out that way. By the time of the July 1997 crisis in Thailand, the consensus had been rejected by many in the region. It had indeed led to the privatization of public assets, increased the flow of FDI, and addressed many of the necessary, but insufficient, technical aspects of economic management. However, overall most Latin Americans deemed it a failure because the reforms did little to improve their daily existence.[11] The first ominous sign of the depth of that rejection came with the democratic election of Colonel Hugo Chávez as president of Venezuela in 1998. A key component of his campaign was a rejection of the Washington consensus and the "savage capitalism" imposed on developing countries by the industrial states.

The various crises created a legitimacy issue for the G-7 and their institutions. A series of books challenged the assumptions of the development models of recent years and called for a complete rethinking of both ideas and institutions.[12] The developing economies became increasingly dubious about the leadership of the West, its multilateral financial institutions, holdovers from the end of World War II, and the argument of "raw," market-driven development. Many developing countries viewed with growing skepticism the mantra that peace, democracy, and free markets would dominate the century. As a global recovery began in the first years of the twenty-first century, old assumptions were cast aside, and recovering countries looked to their own models for growth. Among those taking the lead were Brazil, China, India, and Russia.

After a severe financial crisis in the early 1990s, then finance minister Manmohan Singh of India opened a process of reform and liberalization that continues today.[13] His reelection in 2009 as prime minister should further consolidate the reform process. Deng Xiaoping in China began to allow market forces into agriculture in the late 1970s. That decision unleashed the phenomenon that is China today. The take-off took place under the leadership of Hu Jintao, the paramount leader of the People's Republic of China. His fourth generation of leaders rose to power in 2002 when Hu was chosen as the general secretary of the Communist Party of China.[14] Vladimir Putin became president of Russia in May 2002. The collapse of the Soviet Union in 1991 buried the old communist state but began a decade-long phase of chaos and drift. Putin created a new semi-authoritarian state that restored the country's confidence and opened a period of relative economic stability.[15]

In Brazil, after decades of poor economic management and feckless governance, a turning point took place in 1993–94. Finance Minister Fernando Henrique Cardoso and a team of young reformers introduced a new economic and financial program that promised to control inflation and prepare the country for economic growth. The *Real* Plan—and the name for the new currency—stunned the country, and the world, with its immediate success. It also provided the political platform for the election of Cardoso as Brazil's president at the end of 1994. When his second term ended in 2003, much progress had been made, while many opportunities had been overlooked or missed.

The Goldman Sachs analysis clearly reflected the new trends. As the 2003 Goldman Sachs report pointed out, India's economy could be larger than Japan's by 2032, and China's could be larger than the U.S. economy by 2041 (and larger than everyone else's as early as 2016). The BRICs' economies taken together could be larger than that of the G-6 in 2039. The key assumption of the analysis was that the BRICs would maintain growth-supportive policies that included sound macroeconomic policies and a stable macroeconomic background, strong and stable political institutions, openness, and high levels of education.[16]

But even in 2003, there was caution regarding Brazil's prospects. Compared to China and the other Asian economies, Brazil was much less open to trade, investment and savings were lower, and public and foreign debt were much higher. On the trade question, the tradable goods sector in China was almost eight times larger than that in Brazil, when measured by imports plus exports. Brazilian savings and investment ratios were about 18–19 percent of GDP, at that time, compared to an investment rate of 36 percent of GDP in China and an Asian average of around 30 percent.[17] Goldman Sachs made clear that without a deeper fiscal adjustment and lower ratio of debt to GDP, the private sector was almost completely crowded out from credit markets. China's net foreign debt and public debt were both significantly smaller. Also, 2003 was the first year of the government of President Lula. As we shall see, the transition from Cardoso to the Workers Party government in late 2002 was precarious, with international markets deeply concerned about the possibility of "socialist" antimarket policies in Lula's Brazil. Although he quickly neutralized those fears, in 2003 Lula was still in the process of consolidating his fiscally conservative regime and his support for outward growth strategies.

Between 2003 and 2005, Goldman Sachs noted that updated forecasts suggested that the BRICs' economies could realize the "dream" more quickly than thought in 2003.[18] The case for including this group directly and systematically in global economic policymaking is now overwhelming. The analysis continued:

We see the BRICs as much more than a new emerging-market theme. The BRICs are a key aspect of the modern globalized era. What distinguishes the BRICs from any other story of EM [emerging-market] growth is their ability to influence, and be influenced by, the global economy and global markets in a broad fashion. The current and prospective outlook for globalization has the BRIC nations at its core, and the interplay between the BRICs' economies and the G-7 is a critical aspect of globalization and interdependence. The varied composition among the BRICs, the balance between resource abundance and resource dependence within the BRICs, and the global demographic tilt towards the BRICs allows these economies the chance to participate in an integral way in the world economy.[19]

The 2005 Goldman Sachs report commented that between 2000 and 2005, the BRICs contributed roughly 28 percent of global growth in U.S. dollar terms and 55 percent in purchasing power parity terms. Their share of global trade continued to climb at a rapid rate. At close to 15 percent in 2005, the group had doubled its 2001 level of global trade. According to Goldman Sachs, trade among the BRICs had accelerated, with intra-BRICs trade reaching nearly 8 percent of their total trade in 2005 compared with 5 percent in 2000. By the end of 2005, the BRICs were clearly playing an important role in global financial developments. More recent estimates indicate that the BRICs hold more than 30 percent of world currency reserves, and despite the reserve accumulation, real exchange rates in each country have appreciated over the last few years. Real exchange rate appreciation continues to strengthen their financial position and will account for a significant proportion of their capital accumulation over the next few decades.[20]

The BRICs' current accounts, at the end of 2005, continued to be in surplus and to contribute substantively to the supply of global savings. Goldman Sachs estimated that the BRICs' current accounts would likely be around $240 billion or close to 6 percent of their GDP by the end of 2005. The BRICs' favorable balance of payments is in large part what has allowed the United States to run its current account deficit. The BRICs are increasingly important counterparts to the U.S. current account deficit. Their percentage of total global FDI inflows continued to rise as of 2005 (then about 15 percent of the global total, nearly three times higher than in 2000). At the same time, an even more promising sign of their growing economic relevance was the increase in FDI *outflows* to more than 3 percent of the global total, a sixfold increase since 2000, as BRICs' companies expanded their own global presence.[21]

The BRICs Consolidate

As a consequence of this favorable set of trends, and in the context of rising global growth and demand, the BRICs began to identify issues on which they could coordinate policy. This had little to do with historical or cultural similarities. It had nothing to do with the nature of the political regime in power in each country. Two were dynamic democracies, one was a semiauthoritarian state, and the fourth, China, was a full-fledged communist regime. There was no geographic proximity to unite the four countries. But what drove the convergence of interests, as pointed out by Goldman Sachs, was their simultaneous growth and development in the context of the world economy. As they became more important traders, investors, and interlocutors with the G-7, they began to expect greater respect and higher levels of inclusion in the international policymaking process. An underlying theme of the BRICs' approach to world affairs was a healthy skepticism about the rigidities of the postcommunist world order.

There is not unanimity on every issue. One or more of the BRICs have key issues that drive their search for like-minded allies in the developing world. But by and large, in the first years of the twenty-first century, the four BRICs have become the bellwether for confronting the industrial countries on a wide range of issues, in particular challenging the "old" postcommunist sense that Western-style globalization is inevitable.

Perhaps the first critical issue was that of world trade. A new round of trade discussions began in 2001 in Doha, Qatar. The goal was to launch talks on development, to open markets in agriculture, manufacturing, and services, and to finish the Doha Development Round of negotiations by January 2005. The first two years of talks went relatively well. But in September 2003, in a ministerial meeting in Cancún, Mexico, the developing countries denounced the U.S.–European Union (EU) agricultural proposal as demeaning and created the Bloc of G-20 countries.[22]

The BRIC countries, in particular Brazil, emerged as the key spokesmen and alternative policy formulators for the developing world. Efforts to revive the talks were made in 2005 and 2006, but in July 2006 agricultural subsidies again led to a failure to negotiate a compromise. In June 2007 talks between the United States, the EU, Brazil, and India failed to break the impasse. On July 29, 2008, the Doha round talks failed because of an impasse on farm policies. The United States, India, and China were unable to find a common position. Brazil attempted to broker a compromise, but the positions on both sides became polarized—the United States versus India and China. It would have been difficult, probably impossible, to imagine at a similar meeting ten years ago that two rapidly developing emerging-market states—India and China—would dare to challenge the G-7. It is clear that the fate of any future trade talks will require pragmatic and open negotiations between the BRICs and their allies and not with the United States and the EU.[23]

A similar confrontation took place in L'Aquila, Italy, in July 2009, when the biggest developing nations, again led by the BRICs, refused to commit to specific goals for slashing heat-trapping gases by 2050, undercutting the drive to build a global consensus by the end of 2009 to reverse the threat of climate change. But as reported, "The impasse over the 2050 targets demonstrated again the most vexing problem in reaching a consensus on climate change: the long-standing divisions between developed countries like the United States, Europe, and Japan, on one side, and developing nations like China, India, Brazil, and Mexico, on the other."[24] The L'Aquila standoff was repeated at the December 2009 United Nations climate change talks in Copenhagen. Brazil, China, and India defended the position of the developing countries. They had a major role in drafting the final communiqué, along with the United States and South Africa.

The impasse is a classic standoff between the two groups. While the richest countries have produced the bulk of the pollution blamed for climate change, developing countries are producing increasing volumes of gases. But developing countries say that their path out of poverty should not be halted to fix damage done by the industrial countries. The tensions between the BRICs and other developing states led the United States and the EU to abandon the conference goal of cutting worldwide emissions 50 percent by 2050, with industrial countries cutting theirs 80 percent. But the emerging powers refused to agree because they wanted industrial countries to commit to midterm goals in the next decade and to follow through on promises of financial and technological help for poorer nations.

The L'Aquila summit again opened the door for debate about the appropriate composition of world leadership. Indeed, the G-7 leaders acknowledged that their format was looking outdated in the twenty-first century. The French president, Nicholas Sarkozy, and the Italian prime minister, Silvio Berlusconi, were among those calling for the G-7 to be turned formally into the G-14—taking in Brazil, China, India, Mexico,

South Africa, and Egypt—by the time France takes the chair in 2011. As the meeting in Italy ended, President Sarkozy commented, "It seems unreasonable that the most important international issues are dealt with without Africa, Latin America, and China."[25]

The Financial Crisis

The failures in Geneva in 2008 and in Italy and Denmark in 2009 paralleled the increasing concern of the BRICs with the financial meltdown that began in the United States in 2007–08. There has been an ongoing debate as to whether the developing countries were "coupled" or "decoupled" from the developed world's financial crisis. But as of 2010 it would appear that mild decoupling is the order of the day. A mid-year report commented, "Developing nations shine amid the crisis gloom."[26] The article included a report on the positive stock market performance of the BRICs. It also became clear that the resilient domestic demand of emerging markets, and especially the BRICs, would become a key driver of the export-driven economic recovery of industrial countries over the next few years. It was beginning to look as though the economic balance of power was shifting, especially with forecasts that the BRICs would contribute nearly half of the growth in global consumption by 2010.

The growing concern of the BRICs over the financial crisis led to a series of demands in 2008–09 that they be included in discussions about possible solutions and new policies. The George W. Bush administration, pressured by its EU allies, decided to expand the decisionmaking framework from the traditional G-7 to the G-20, to include the largest economies in the world.[27] Brazil quickly emerged as a prolocutor for the emerging-market economies that would be included in the G-20. The BRICs played an active role in the first meeting in November 2008 in Washington and the second one in London in April 2009. The declaration of the "Summit on Financial Markets and the World Economy, November 15, 2008," clearly reflects the sense of urgency of the BRICs in calling for strengthening transparency and accountability, enhancing sound regulation, promoting integrity in financial markets, reinforcing international cooperation, and reforming international financial institutions.[28] The declaration addressed directly the criticism of the BRIC states when it commented, "Major underlying factors to the current situation were, among others, inconsistent and insufficiently coordinated macroeconomic policies [and] inadequate structural reforms, which led to unsustainable global macroeconomic outcomes. These developments, together, contributed to excesses and ultimately resulted in severe market disruption."[29]

The London meeting on April 2, 2009, produced the "Global Plan for Recovery and Reform."[30] It emphasized restoring growth and jobs, strengthening financial supervision and regulation, strengthening global financial institutions, resisting protectionism, promoting global trade and investment, and ensuring a fair and sustainable recovery for all. Prior to the April 2009 summit in London, the countries' finance ministers had convened outside of London for preliminary talks. At the conclave, the four BRIC states issued a separate, joint declaration outlining their vision for how world leaders should respond to the crisis. They called for reform of the IMF as well as additional funding for the institution; they stated that the current system of choosing the leaders of the World Bank and the IMF must change (the United States chooses the head of the World Bank and the Europeans choose the managing director of the IMF), and they called for improved information sharing from the industrial countries.

In September 2009 a third G-20 meeting took place in Pittsburgh, Pennsylvania. It was clear that the BRIC countries had become prominent interlocutors with the G-7 in preparing the agenda for the meetings and in reviewing the action to date on the communiqués from prior summits in Washington and London and from consequent consultations. Moreover, the successful interventions of the London summit in halting worldwide economic decline reinforced the relative power of this body. The Pittsburgh summit addressed key issues such as global stimulus packages, financial market regulations, compensation, and energy security, resolving to work together to establish "internationally agreed" financial regulations.[31] For the first time, each country agreed to undergo a "peer review" from other member countries as well as monitoring by the International Monetary Fund.[32]

One of the most important outcomes for the BRIC countries was the agreement to modernize the infrastructure of global economic cooperation. This would shift at least 5 percent of IMF quotas from "overrepresented" countries to "underrepresented" ones, in order to reflect the relative weights of emerging markets in the world economy.[33] Similarly, there would be a 3 percent increase in voting power of developing and transition countries within the World Bank, "reflecting countries' evolving economic weight and the World Bank's development mission."[34] It thus appeared that the economic strength of the BRICs would be matched with decisionmaking power in global institutions. Finally, the group resolved to convene annual meetings of member countries starting in 2009. The G-20 would become the principal instrument for worldwide economic cooperation, replacing the G-7.

The BRIC Summit

The first summits of the BRIC countries were held in Yekaterinburg, Russia, in May 2008 and June 2009. The meetings were a logical follow-up to the increasing consultation among the four countries on policy issues of common concern. The four countries constitute about 15 percent of global output and, perhaps more important, about 40 percent of global currency reserves.[35] The summits were in part a symbol of the growing frustration with the U.S. dollar's status as the world's reserve currency, which enables Washington to run budget deficits without risking the kind of budgetary day of reckoning that other countries risk.[36]

While there have been periodic complaints about the dollar through the years, the criticisms from the BRIC countries have become more frequent and more acerbic lately, including calls for a supranational currency to replace the dollar. In March 2009 the prime minister of China, Wen Jiabao, expressed concerns about U.S. budget deficits, suggesting that they might lead to inflation and a weaker dollar, either of which would hurt China's $1 trillion investment in American government debt.[37] Later that month, the head of China's central bank called for a new international currency to replace the dollar.[38]

For Russia, undermining the dollar as the prevailing medium of exchange reflects a broader Russian belief that the United States exercises a dominance in global affairs that exceeds its diminishing power. Representing nationalist sentiment in Brazil, former strategic affairs minister Roberto Mangabeira Unger commented, "The world economy should not remain entangled, so directly and unnecessarily, in the vicissitudes of a single great world power. The developing countries should not have to see painfully accumulated hard-currency reserves fall under the shadow of major devaluations."[39]

But the realities were clear as the summits convened. China, whose economy dwarfs those of the other three BRIC countries, depends on the export of manufactured goods to the United States and Europe. Russia sells oil, natural gas, and other natural resources abroad. Brazil focuses on agricultural exports, while India's growth has been based largely on its domestic market. The four countries do not necessarily do much business with one another. Only 2 percent of China's trade last year was with Russia. At the same time, Brazil announced this year that China had surpassed the United States as its largest trading partner and said in May 2009 that the government would look for ways to finance Brazilian trade without the dollar.

At the summit in Russia in June 2009, the four leaders issued a joint statement: "The emerging and developing economies must have greater voice and representation in international financial institutions. There is a strong need for a stable, predictable, and more diversified international monetary system."[40] The leaders issued a final communiqué that again called for greater participation for the developing economies in global decisionmaking. They also called for comprehensive reform of the United Nations to deal with global challenges more effectively and give Brazil and India a greater role. The BRIC leaders also discussed global food and energy security and measures to prevent climate change. The group will meet formally in Brazil in 2010, after informal consultations made during the September 2009 G-20 summit in Pittsburgh.

The BRICs in Context

The BRIC acronym appears to be here to stay. The world order is changing, but very slowly. Adjustments will need to be made, but probably with great caution and patience. The four BRIC countries are not an entirely coherent group, but they have come to embody twenty-first-century skepticism with markets and with institutions that date from the 1940s. As a recent *Financial Times* editorial stated,

> It would be wrong to be cynical. Other groups, too, are riddled with contradictions and competing objectives. The global financial crisis does provide an opportunity to challenge a world order too long dominated by rich countries often serving their own interests. The BRICs are right to demand a greater say in bodies where Europe is overrepresented such as the United Nations and the International Monetary Fund. They are right, too, to suggest alternatives to the world's overdependence on dollars.[41]

The *Financial Times* editorial concludes that the BRIC bloc "is, indeed, an acronym in search of a purpose. But it is also a bit like God. If Jim O'Neill had not invented it, someone else would have had to."[42]

Just twenty years ago, it would have been very difficult to imagine that Brazil would emerge as a BRIC. The following chapters provide the background and context for Brazil's achievement of that status. Brazil's ascension to the international scene is even more surprising considering its late-comer status and relative lack of importance within the far-flung Portuguese empire in the sixteenth century. Its prominence, over the centuries, has been due to its ability to provide raw materials and commodities for the world markets. Sugar, chocolate, gold, diamonds, rubber, and coffee dominated, at various times, the economic profile of the country. But compared to some of its neighbors in Spanish America, Brazil was a sprawling, decentralized colony. Institutions emerged late and were weak. Slowly between 1500, the year of discovery, and 1750, the date of the Treaty of Madrid, Brazil's boundaries expanded to occupy half of the South American continent. But the nation occupied the coast; the interior was not "opened" until well into the twentieth century. Socially, Brazil could not be more different from its neighbors. While the Spaniards found large indigenous populations that they exploited for cheap labor, the Portuguese imported slaves from Africa to work the plantations. This led, over time, to a mulatto population formed through miscegenation.

Again, in contrast to its neighbors, Brazil achieved independence in 1822 as an empire, not a republic. It avoided the civil wars that divided Spanish America for decades after rejecting Spanish rule. The empire was dominated by landed elites who maintained social and political control under the umbrella of the imperial family based in Rio de Janeiro. The empire ended, without conflict, in 1889. Slavery had been legally abolished in 1888. For many wealthy Brazilians the institution of slavery and the imperial order were linked, and the empire made little sense without that linkage to a colonial past. The old republic (1889–1930) was a highly decentralized state dominated by local political clans. Key was federal support for coffee grown primarily in the booming southern state of São Paulo. Internal conflicts led to the collapse of the republic in 1930, again peacefully, and the arrival in power of the dominant figure in Brazilian politics in the first half of the twentieth century, Getúlio Vargas.

Vargas, from the southern state of Rio Grande do Sul, centralized political power in the hands of the federal government in Rio de Janeiro. He presided over a new elite of public sector servants, middle-class professionals, and coffee entrepreneurs. Refusing to cede power, he closed the political system, with the support of the armed forces, in 1937. His government also took the decision to support the United States and its allies in World War II. Brazil was the only country in the hemisphere to send a fighting force to Europe to join the Allied war effort. Vargas was removed, without incident, from office in 1945. The first "modern" general elections, with competitive political parties, were held in that year, with the new government taking office in 1946. The next eighteen years witnessed a rapid process of import substitution industrialization, which was very successful in some industries, but not in others. The program, combined with the building of a new capital city in the interior, Brasília, led to hyperinflation, mismanagement, and political polarization. The confrontation between radical reformers and the country's establishment ended with the overthrow of the weak, democratic regime in 1964.

The military and its civilian supporters governed Brazil from 1964 to 1985. The import substitution industrialization program was deepened. A national highway system was constructed. Brasília became the de jure capital of the country. But security forces were responsible for widespread human rights abuses, and the authoritarian system came under growing pressure in the early 1980s to plan a return to democratic government; it took place in 1985. The new president, Tancredo Neves, took ill and died before his inauguration, to be replaced by his ill-prepared and unpopular vice president. The next decade was one of failed efforts to control fiscal spending. It saw various unsuccessful adjustment programs. Only with the decision to introduce a new currency and an orthodox adjustment program in 1993–94, under the leadership of Finance Minister Fernando Henrique Cardoso, did the Brazilian economy stop the freefall of the previous decades. As a result of the *Real* Plan, the first signs of a new Brazil became visible. Cardoso undertook important reforms, but the government was hit by the contagion from the financial crises of 1997–98 and was forced to devalue the currency in January 1999. With further reforms supported by Congress, the economy returned to sluggish growth in the last years of the president's second term of office.

The critical turning point came with the election in 2002 of Lula. Headed by the leader and co-founder of the Workers Party, the Lula administration confounded international markets with a straight-forward orthodox fiscal program. As Goldman Sachs was creating the BRIC acronym, Lula and his financial team were laying the groundwork for the impressive macroeconomic management that has characterized the country since his inauguration. Inflation targeting, responsible fiscal federalism, important progress in reducing poverty, export diversification, and myriad other innovations have characterized the Lula years. Recent petroleum discoveries indicate that the country will be an energy giant within a decade, and the sugar-based ethanol program provides another important energy resource. A robust partnership with China has provided an important market for Brazil's exports. China's impressive levels of economic growth required the commodities and raw materials that Brazil possesses in abundance, and high international prices for exports such as iron ore and soybeans benefited Brazil's reserve levels. The relationship was complementary: China had the capacity to pay for what it needed, and Brazil was a reliable source of the inputs for China's growth. And as a result of the performance of Lula's government, all of the rating agencies have given Brazil an investment-grade rating.[43]

The ensuing chapters lay out the long and often "stop-go" history of Brazil's modernization. The impressive turnaround after 1994 often astounds analysts—and Brazilians. The decisions taken since 1994, and consolidated since 2002, have provided the sound underpinnings that give this vibrant democracy the right to take its place next to China, India, and Russia as the twenty-first-century BRIC nation-states. While the BRIC countries have great levels of disparity, diplomatically they have come to represent a defining moment as old institutions adapt to the new century and greater "space" is opened for new players. That process will be complex and will take longer than many now suspect. But the debates surrounding changes in the global system—economic and political—will inevitably include the BRICs.

2

The Historical Background:
Colony, Empire, and Republic

Portugal did not conquer Brazil, as Spain did its empire. After the discovery, it took decades for the Portuguese to understand the potential of their new colony. Unlike Spanish America, Brazil's institutional development was slow and erratic. With Napoleon's invasion of the Iberian Peninsula in the early 1800s, the Portuguese royal family fled to Brazil, and the Spanish court was captured by the conqueror. At independence in the early decades of the nineteenth century, Spanish America splintered into individual republics; Brazil maintained a monarchical regime and did not splinter. The end of the empire in 1889 and the creation of a republic led to regional domination by the two most powerful states; the other provinces were left to their own devices.

The collapse of the first republic in 1930 and the rise to power of Getúlio Vargas led to a centralization of state authority and the beginnings of industrialization. In 1937 Vargas closed the democratic process and ruled as a strongman until 1945. The republic was reestablished in 1946, only to collapse in 1964 as a result of economic chaos and political polarization. A military government ruled from 1964 to 1985. With the end of the authoritarian regime, democracy was restored. The transition was not an easy one, and it was not until 1994 that a profound economic transformation stabilized the economy and prepared Brazil to emerge as an important international player in the twenty-first century.

Brazilian and international scholars have written some excellent histories of Brazil's discovery and colonization.[1] Rather than attempt to replicate them, this chapter summarizes the principal historical and cultural turning points or transitions that are essential to understanding the country's development.

Brazil's Colonial Experience

First and foremost, the discovery and colonization of Brazil by the Portuguese were very different from the experience of Spain and its soon-to-be empire in Mexico and on the Pacific side of the South American continent. These territories quickly became the epicenter of Spanish imperial expansion in the sixteenth century. The conquest of the Inca and Mayan empires yielded enormous wealth and was an indication of much more to be found. With the discovery of the great silver mine in Potosí, Bolivia, the wealth of Spanish America was confirmed and soon exploited through reliance on the large indigenous population, which the colonizers subjugated and enslaved.

In contrast, Brazil was almost an afterthought for the seagoing Portuguese, who were much more interested in India and Africa. Portugal's claim to the New World resulted more from its traditional overseas trade rivalry with Spain than from a desire for a South American colony. When Christopher Columbus reached America in 1492, he thought he had reached the China Sea. Portugal, in defense of its maritime and mercantilist interests, contested the Spanish claim to the territory Columbus had discovered. The diplomatic conflict was resolved through the Treaty of Tordesillas in 1494. The Vatican divided the world into two hemispheres separated by an imaginary line, giving the territory west of the line to Spain and the portion east of the border to Portugal. This settlement gave Portugal a relatively small portion of the South American continent, a disadvantage that would be remedied over the next 250 years.

The first natural resource yielded by Portugal's new colony was brazilwood or *pau-brasil,* which the nomadic Indian inhabitants collected and traded with the Portuguese. Due to its early economic importance, the tree eventually gave its name to half the continent. However, other economic interests soon took form. As rivalry among the European powers, including England and France, intensified in the sixteenth century, the government in Lisbon decided to protect its interests by colonizing the newly discovered territory. A three-year expedition led by Martim Afonso de Sousa established a colony at São Vicente on the southeast coast in 1532.

Dom João III, the Portuguese monarch, then made an important decision: he decided to create hereditary captaincies.[2] Fifteen land divisions were plotted running parallel to the equator and ending at the Line of Tordesillas, which was still ill-defined. The donataries, who were all connected to the royal court in some way, were given the responsibility for settlement. They were given possession of the land, but not the right to take ownership. The intent of the Portuguese monarchy was to retain ultimate control over the colony, even though it did not have the resources to develop it—the captaincy concept was a way to foster colonization with private resources. The captaincy experiment failed: only two of the original settlements—São Vicente and Pernambuco on the northeast coast—prospered, but it established a pattern of settlement by large landed estates that dominated Brazilian land use, history, and politics for centuries. As Celso Furtado, one of Brazil's most eminent economic historians, has argued, the prevalence of large estates was in sharp contrast to the pattern of settlement in North America. Over the centuries, the survival of this form of settlement contributed to income inequality, limited the internal market, and maintained a strict division between haves and have-nots.[3]

The creation of large and increasingly autonomous land holdings was the first in a series of factors that decisively shaped Brazil's development. The second was the weakness of the royal administrative presence. The first governor general arrived in 1545, accompanied by a small contingent of Jesuits. But Brazil's administrative center, located on the northeast coast in the city of Salvador, remained a weak and distant presence as the colony began to consolidate in the mid-1500s. Unlike the Spanish conquest, which was characterized by the strong interdependent presence of the "cross" and the "sword," Brazilian settlement took on a haphazard and unplanned trajectory. Communication among the captaincies was difficult given the terrain and vast distances involved. The royal administrative staff was small and isolated. Without a large military contingent, as in Spanish America, the civilian governors were mostly—although not entirely—symbolic during the first century of settlement. However, the situation began to change slowly with the discovery of minerals in the center-south, in and around the state of Minas Gerais in the early eighteenth century. Portuguese supervision became stricter in order to guarantee that revenues from the operation of the mines were returned to Lisbon.[4]

A third important factor was the need to identify a workforce for the colony. The nomadic Indian populations the Portuguese encountered were not susceptible to organization, as in the Spanish empire. They quickly disappeared into the forests or were decimated by disease and repression. The labor issue became acute when it was discovered that sugar, increasingly in demand in developing Europe, could be grown easily and rapidly on the humid coast of the northeast. Having become a leader in the slave trade in Africa during the fifteenth century, Portugal chose to solve the labor shortage in its new colony with a "product" it knew notoriously well. Between the mid-sixteenth century and 1855 when the slave trade ceased, more than 4 million slaves entered Brazil.

As in the United States, African slavery helped to define and demarcate the social and class lines of Brazilian society for centuries. Moreover, it created a mythology that has been difficult to challenge until recent years. Many in Brazil have argued that slavery was more benign in Brazil than in countries like the United States, that the relations between masters and slaves were less cruel and repressive, and that miscegenation, typically between male owners and slave women, created a "cosmic nation" in the tropics, the foundation on which a new social entity would be built.[5] In fact, as Anthony Marx argues in a pioneering study, Brazilian elites were ingenious in addressing the issue of slavery. No explicit racial divide was created as in the United States and South Africa; rather, through the process of miscegenation, a mulatto race emerged with the intermarriage of white settlers and African women. While slaves in Brazil were treated as harshly as in those two countries, local elites succeeded in convincing the slave population that their place was in a natural order of things given the mixing of the races, and, therefore, protest was unnecessary (and probably futile). This successful manipulation of the black and mixed-race population continued even after abolition in 1888 and helps to explain, even today, the inability of people of color to unite.[6]

Only in the late twentieth century did the federal government recognize that Afro-Brazilian citizens were the subjects of inequality and discrimination. President Fernando Henrique Cardoso (1994–2002) and President Luiz Inácio (Lula) da Silva (2002–10) sponsored social development programs that have begun to address marginalized Brazilians of color. It remains to be seen whether greater social status will lead to an explicit political movement based on race, as has begun to occur in some of the Andean countries like Bolivia, where indigenous political movements are now in power.

A fourth reality that helped to define colonial Brazil was its dependence on natural and mineral resources. Sugar led the way in the mid-1500s. Indeed, Brazil was the world's largest supplier of sugar by the early seventeenth century, and the sugar industry made Brazil central to Portugal's failing fortunes as its empire declined. The sugar plantation boom was followed by the discovery of gold and diamonds in the central plateau at the end of the seventeenth century. In addition, there were small booms and busts in cotton and cacao from time to time.

A fifth and final consideration must be the transformation of Brazil from a relatively small portion of South America into the dominant presence in half of the continent. Brazil's size is an important part of the country's image, for better and for worse. For its Spanish American neighbors, the expansion of Portuguese Brazil was a continual threat to their own territorial integrity—a perception that lingered into the twentieth century. For Brazilians, the country's expansion was the logical culmination of a dynamic people's search for its identity, a process that had begun in the mid-1600s when Portuguese colonists drove off incursions by the Dutch, particularly in the northeast.

Both private and public efforts played a role in the rapid expansion of the colony between 1500 and 1750, when its new borders were recognized by the Treaty of Madrid. (This ruling was often challenged in succeeding years, but, by and large, it defined the general outlines of modern Brazil.) Private expansion originated in the region known as São Vicente (which is today's São Paulo) in the southeast area of the colony. As cotton and wheat farming and cattle ranching became increasingly important activities at the end of the 1600s, local settlers began to explore the formerly untouched hinterland north and west of São Paulo. The Paulistas, as they became known, began to move south in search of mining opportunities. These expeditions were characterized by personalist flags or *bandeiras*. Each year large sorties moved into the interior in search of slaves, gold, new ground for cattle development, and related activities. The success of the Paulista activity led to the creation in 1711 of an independent city named São Paulo on the southeast coast of the colony. At the same time, the crown dispatched naval expeditions to explore the Amazon River and its tributaries. The combined effect, over a number of years, was to push Spanish claims back over the Andean mountain chain and to give Brazil its current territorial outline.

The interaction of these five historical realities shaped the Portuguese experience in the New World. First, strong, assertive families and clans that were a world unto themselves came to control large tracts of land in Brazil's northeast, providing a paradigm for later settlement. Second, the weakness and relative passivity of the colonial government strengthened the local clans' right to rule. Third, the creation of a workforce based on imported African slaves, not native labor, set the tone for Brazil's social and economic development for the next two-and-a-half centuries. Fourth, dependence on natural resources became and remained the country's economic model well into the twentieth century. And finally, the expansion of the colony's borders consolidated Brazil's potential as a great power.

The development of an independent Brazilian identity was supported by the continued decline of Portugal. The King of Spain occupied the Portuguese throne between 1580 and 1640. Increasingly, the relationship between Portugal and its largest colony was driven by Brazil's ability to provide a steady stream of income for a decadent former power largely isolated on the edge of Europe. Reform efforts were undertaken from time to time in Lisbon to better integrate Brazil into the surviving Portuguese mercantilist system, but with limited results.

As the colonial period wound down, Brazil was not a sophisticated colony when compared to imperial centers like Mexico City or Lima. Unlike Spain, Portugal had not promoted universities or allowed printing presses, fearing the creation of an enlightened or at least a literate elite, and the controversial decision in the 1750s to expel the Jesuits severely damaged what little educational infrastructure the colony had. Rural plantation owners dominated the social order, supported by a large slave population, followed by a mixed bag of merchants, bureaucrats, clergy, and artisans. The social scene was further complicated as time went on by a large pool of freed slaves in the urban centers. While inroads had been made in exploring the interior of the country, Brazil remained a basically coastal society with only fragments of understanding regarding the inland portions of the country.

By the end of the 1700s, Brazilians had increasingly begun to disassociate themselves from Portugal. This trend was accelerated by two developments that set the scene for Brazilian independence in 1822. The first was the wave of revolutions that shook the traditional European powers—the American War of Independence in 1776 and the French Revolution in 1789. These events inspired the emergence of new ideas and new local leaders in Brazil and ultimately a series of dramatic but failed efforts to declare independence from Portugal. The second crucial development was Napoleon Bonaparte's decision to invade the Iberian Peninsula in late 1807. Urged on by Great Britain, which had been Portugal's major trading partner since the seventeenth century, the regent, Prince João, decided to move the entire court to Brazil. In November 1807, under British naval protection, the government abandoned Lisbon for the New World. In contrast, the Spanish royal family was taken hostage by Napoleon.

This event was unprecedented in the history of European colonialism. While there had been discussions in Lisbon for many years regarding a transfer to the New World to restore the vigor of the dynasty, nothing had been done until events forced the monarchy's hand. The Napoleonic invasion triggered a historic move that led to the opening of Brazil's ports to friendly nations, such as England. London benefited immediately from this shift, as did Rio de Janeiro, which became the port of entry for manufactured goods for both Brazil and other South American markets. In addition, Dom João's presence in Rio de Janeiro (1808–21) changed the colony dramatically. Books and ideas circulated. Theaters and libraries appeared for the first time. Brazil became a favorite destination for European travelers.

After Napoleon's defeat in 1814, Dom João, who succeeded to the throne in 1816, and the court were expected to return to Lisbon. They did not, but pressure to do so intensified after a liberal revolution in Portugal in 1820. The revolutionaries, to restore legitimacy to the regime, demanded the return of the king. Fearing the loss of his throne, João VI departed Brazil in April 1821, leaving his son, Pedro, behind as prince regent. Political currents in Lisbon quickly turned against the autonomy that Brazil had enjoyed since 1808. Rather than accept a rollback of Brazil's status, the "Brazilian" faction in Rio de Janeiro urged independence; the prince regent agreed and declared the colony free of Portuguese rule on September 7, 1822. At twenty-four years of age, he was crowned as Brazil's first emperor.

This peaceful transition to independence contrasts dramatically with the bloody collapse of the Spanish American empire at the same time. Brazil's formal independence and the guarantee of its territorial integrity were accomplished relatively easily with British military and commercial support and the quick granting of diplomatic recognition by countries like the United States. But independence did not solve the many internal problems that faced the new empire and its fledgling government.

The Imperial Experiment

Four issues dominated the political life of the empire until its demise in 1889.[7] The first and critical challenge was creating a suitable political framework for the country that clarified the role of the emperor and the imperial court. The second challenge was managing relations between the center, in Rio de Janeiro, and the sprawling periphery. Given the legacy of slavery and mounting international pressure to abolish the institution, the third challenge was the need to define an appropriate social model for the empire. Finally, the government faced the task of promoting economic growth. Policymakers debated pressing questions: Did the government need to diversify the national economy? If so, what were the alternatives? Were they feasible, given the status of landownership, the labor market, and the patterns of international trade? England, the pioneer of the industrial revolution, was already in a preferred position to supply Brazil with manufactured goods, which reduced local incentives to invest in industry. And the situation was unlikely to change in the absence of a native commercial class with the potential to offset the power of large landowners.

Institutional Challenges

The central political question in the early 1820s was the distribution of power between Dom Pedro I and the legislature. Elections for a constituent assembly were held in late 1822, with a very limited electorate,[8] and the assembly convened in May 1823. Unable to reach compromise with the assembly, the court faction dissolved the body and promulgated its own constitution in March 1824. This document, which remained the basic constitutional framework of Brazil until the end of the empire, included guarantees of individual liberty and rights. However, it also reserved a great deal of formal power for the emperor. Both houses of the Congress—the Chamber of Deputies and the Senate—were elected, but voting was highly restricted and indirect. Those eligible to vote chose the members of an electoral college, who elected the members of the Chamber of Deputies. For the Senate, three candidates were elected from each province, and the emperor chose which of them would be appointed for life. The emperor also appointed the presidents of the provinces. An interesting innovation, borrowed from French political theory, was the concept of the "moderating power" of the emperor. While not interfering in the day-to-day administrative affairs of the state, the emperor had the authority to "moderate" among factions at times of tension or crisis. Together with his constitutional prerogatives to appoint senators, dissolve the Chamber of Deputies, and approve or veto decisions of the legislature, this authority made the emperor the key political operative in the new constitutional framework.

In Rio de Janeiro tensions soon arose between the mainly Portuguese supporters of the young emperor—the absolutists—and a growing liberal faction. The conflict deepened until the emperor was forced to abdicate on April 7, 1831, in favor of his five-year-old son, Dom Pedro II. Pedro I returned to Europe and never visited Brazil again. A regent was installed to govern on behalf of the young emperor until he came of age. Under the weak regency, elites clashed over questions such as the appropriate role of the government in Rio, the amount of autonomy provincial political leaders should have, and the privileged status of Portuguese citizens who remained after the hasty departure of the first emperor.

Gradually, structures of consolidation began to emerge. Two new parties—the Conservatives and the Liberals—came to dominate the political stage. The Conservatives generally had the support of the national bureaucrats, rural landowners in the major states of Rio de Janeiro, Pernambuco, and Bahia, and the established merchant class; the opposition drew strength from the small urban class and rural landowners from the less conservative provinces of São Paulo, Rio Grande do Sul, and Minas Gerais. However, the differences between the two groups were not overly significant. The major differences were over how centralized political power should be, whether the right to vote should be extended to a wider segment of society, and the defense of individual liberties.

In an effort to build a national government, and to avoid further conflict and polarization, Dom Pedro II was declared emperor at the age of fourteen in July 1840, putting the period of regency to an end. Institutionalization moved more rapidly after the boy-emperor was crowned. The emperor was given the authority in 1847 to appoint the new president of the Council of Ministers. The emperor also began to use his moderating power when the Chamber of Deputies did not agree with his cabinet appointments. After consulting with the Council of State (composed of life appointees designated by the emperor), Pedro would dissolve the Chamber of Deputies and call for new elections. In addition, the two political parties matured; policy differences were stark at times, but settled without conflict. The system functioned reasonably well since both parties preferred preserving the rules of the game to undermining them with moves that might produce unforeseen consequences.

Territorial Challenges

Until the empire began to consolidate in the 1850s, territorial disputes plagued the new nation. There were ongoing rural protests in the northeastern provinces and efforts to reject the empire, especially in the province of Pernambuco, until the late 1840s. At one point, the far north-ern province of Pará attempted to declare independence, an effort that failed, but at great cost. The situation was no more settled in the south. In the 1820s Brazil became engaged in a costly and unsuccessful war with Argentina over possession of what would become the independent state of Uruguay, a "buffer" zone between the two antagonists in the South-ern Cone. Then in 1835 a rebellion broke out in the southernmost province of Rio Grande do Sul, which was socially and politically closer to Argentina and Uruguay than to Brazil. The rebellion among the gau-chos, as the province's residents were known, ended with a negotiated settlement in 1845 that left Rio Grande do Sul to play an "outrider" role in the empire—and later in the republic—for many years to come.

The danger posed by these territorial disputes was exacerbated by the weakness and indiscipline of the incipient Brazilian army, which relied largely on poor and uneducated recruits. To improve security, in 1840 the government established a national guard to replace the old local militias. The army remained weak until the War of the Triple Alliance in the 1860s. The guard was controlled by the local, landed elites to maintain order in the provinces and soon became a formidable bastion of the elite.

Social and Economic Challenges

By the 1850s the empire was coming into its own. But economic and demographic changes soon began to undermine the imperial system. The main force driving these changes was the rise of coffee, which became Brazil's principal export item.[9] Cultivation moved quickly from the Paraiba valley between Rio and São Paulo to São Paulo State in the 1870s. The expansion was directly supported by the arrival of British capital and engineers, who built the first railroad to connect the coffee zones and the emerging port of Santos. By 1894 Brazil had become the world's most important coffee export center (see table 2-1).

The rise of coffee had significant implications for Brazil's develop-ment. On the social side, the new coffee growers began to employ free laborers and to support European immigration. Many, although not all, planters believed that the "decadent" slave class was inappropriate for the new dynamics of export-led coffee production—the remaining slave population was growing old, was uneducated, and represented the back-ward rural Brazil of the past. This view was linked to two other concerns: first, that Brazil could not become a competitive and modern nation-state if it remained the last country in the world to abolish slavery as a formal

TABLE 2-1. Brazilian Exports in the Nineteenth Century

Percent of exports

Time period	Coffee	Sugar	Cocoa	Cotton
1821–30	18.4	30.1	0.5	20.6
1831–40	43.8	24.0	0.6	10.8
1841–50	41.4	26.7	1.0	7.5
1851–60	48.8	21.2	1.0	6.2
1861–70	45.5	12.3	0.9	18.3
1871–80	56.6	11.8	1.2	9.5
1881–90	61.5	9.9	1.6	4.2
1891–1900	64.5	6.0	1.5	2.7

Source: Hélio S. Silva, "Tendências e características do comércio exterior no século XIX," *Revista de História da Economia Brasileira* 1, no. 1 (June 1953): 8.

institution and, second, that Brazil would not be accepted as a serious contender in world affairs unless it was perceived as a white nation. Immigration was seen as the solution to these problems. By increasing the availability of European workers, immigration would reduce the need for slave labor and increase profitability in the coffee industry by importing what was believed to be a stronger work ethic. In addition, increasing white immigration would help to dilute the results of centuries of miscegenation.[10] However, in practice, the treatment of the newly arrived Europeans was harsh, leading to protests by both immigrants and their native governments. This attitude would change over time, but it provided a less than welcoming environment for early immigrants.

On the political side, the rise of both coffee and the province of São Paulo began a slow but clear trend in support of decentralization and provincial autonomy. In addition, the new coffee elites and their allies began to question the need for the empire if it was to retain a backward, centralized, and relatively inflexible system of governance. Would a republican form of government, as found in all of Brazil's neighbors, be more suitable to a modern nation-state?

The End of the Empire

These complicated and intertwined philosophical, political, and social issues became increasingly salient in the 1880s as power relationships within Brazil began to shift. As the province of São Paulo moved to the front of the pecking order in terms of economic power, its political leadership, like that of neighboring Minas Gerais, began to seek greater "space" at the center of the system. In contrast to the old northeastern sugar barons, who had played a much more passive role during the colonial period, the coffee elites understood the importance of access to political power to ensure public policy decisions in favor of their regional economic interests. As coffee rose in importance, the new entrepreneurs became power brokers on a national scale. São Paulo and Minas Gerais became infamous as the *café com leite* (coffee and milk) states that dominated the economy and the political system until 1930.

These developments were paralleled by the growth within the armed forces of pressures for renewal and modernization. New ideas about military training and education began to enter Brazil from Europe in the 1870s. New military institutions were established, and an updated curriculum based on "order and progress" became popular among the military leadership. The officer corps became increasingly concerned about the future of both its institution and the country as a whole. In June 1887 it established the Clube Militar to defend the interests of the armed forces.

Against this changing economic and political landscape, the issue of slavery rose to the top of the agenda. External pressure to abolish slavery came from both Britain and the United States, following the end of the civil war, and internal support for the institution was on the decline. Provincial groups that had long supported slavery as a suitable workforce in early coffee-growing regions such as the Paraiba valley—located between Rio de Janeiro and São Paulo and the center of coffee production—had less interest in defending it once coffee production and power moved west to São Paulo Province. Northern and northeastern slave owners became increasingly ambivalent. Once legislation in the 1870s prohibited the import of slaves, an aging slave population had less and less appeal to many owners.

The new bourgeoisie in São Paulo and their regional allies were, to say the least, disdainful of being identified with a disreputable social policy of the old regime and found the solution to their labor needs in European immigration. In particular, the unification and economic modernization of Italy prompted many poor peasant families to move overseas. Paulista elites, after a poor start in attracting and retaining immigrants, adopted policies of subsidized transportation and housing that made the region a favored destination for European workers.

Fueled by this confluence of forces, the domestic abolitionist movement led by elite figures like Joaquim Nabuco from Pernambuco grew in importance. In 1888 Princess Isabel, the heir of the aging emperor Dom Pedro II (who was receiving medical treatment in Italy at the time), signed the Golden Law, which abolished slavery as a national institution. But this reform was not enough to satisfy those pressing for change. The republican idea was becoming increasingly attractive. The old imperial elite appeared trapped in the past and locked in conflict with both the Catholic Church and the armed forces. While the emperor continued to command respect, Princess Isabel and her French consort were widely unpopular.

The movement in favor of a republic steadily gathered strength. In November 1889 Marshal Deodoro da Fonseca, a senior figure in the armed forces, agreed to lead a movement to remove the emperor. Faced with the proclamation of a republic, the emperor offered no resistance and quietly left Brazil, with his family, for exile in Europe.[11] The difficult process of regime creation again confronted the political and military elite.

The legacy of the imperial experiment was not impressive. While constitutional rule had been established, it was fragile. Vast differences in power and influence existed across the half-continent. While slavery as an institution had been closed, its social and economic ramifications continued to haunt succeeding regimes. And while coffee had replaced sugar as the dominant crop, the sources of economic and political power in Brazil remained as concentrated as ever. Some felt nostalgia for the imperial regime. The emperor was an admired figure both at home and abroad. He and the government had prevented the splintering of Brazil into smaller units. Early separatist efforts in the 1820s and 1830s had been resolved relatively peacefully. While Brazil did not industrialize during the empire, the coffee industry became an important source of national revenue, and urbanization began to supplant the old rural towns.

The Old Republic

The end of the empire, while abrupt, transpired quietly and without violence, leaving the military and civilian elites to struggle with the question of what to do next. Initially the outlook for agreement appeared poor. The "big three" states of São Paulo, Minas Gerais, and Rio Grande do Sul, the economic and political drivers of Brazil, favored a federal arrangement that would give them as much autonomy as possible. But even within these three states there were philosophical differences. The military, the critical player in November 1889, was also fragmented. The traditionalists wanted a strong army but did not have a broader vision for the new government. Deodoro da Fonseca was suspected by both military and civilian elites of desiring to establish a strong personalist regime; the best antidote, they thought, was to call a constituent assembly to draft a new constitution.

The new constitution announced in February 1891 established a liberal federal republic. The states were given the power to borrow abroad and to create their own military forces. They were also given the power to charge taxes on their exports, which guaranteed a source of revenue that supported de facto autonomy. These prerogatives were especially important to the powerful state of São Paulo. The central government, located in Rio de Janeiro, controlled import taxes and commanded the national armed forces. Rio de Janeiro also retained the right to intervene in the states to preserve order. In a significant break with the past, the two houses of the national legislature were directly elected. Direct and universal suffrage was established with no financial requirements. Church and state were separated. And in an important measure to deal with the continuing flow of European immigrants, a law decreed on November 15, 1889, gave automatic citizenship to all foreigners in Brazil as of that date.

One reality did not change: the dependence on primary sector exports, of which coffee remained predominant. Since the 1850s, some progress had been made in developing a textile industry, but the nation's economic model remained rooted in the past. While at the end of the empire some investments had been made in physical infrastructure—ports and railroads in particular—they were constructed principally to support the export sector. One positive development was the gradual emergence of a salaried class of consumers, stimulated by the end of slavery and the advent of large-scale immigration.

The continuing dependence on primary sector exports limited the new government's ability to address its precarious financial situation. The debt it inherited from the empire soaked up a significant portion of Brazil's foreign exchange earnings, which were generated largely by coffee sales. Since coffee pricing was not in the government's hands, state finances remained turbulent throughout the old republic.

Despite these struggles, Brazil's new leaders worked hard to project the image abroad of a serious, modern nation-state. A good deal of the success of this venture was due to the indefatigable diplomacy of the baron of Rio Branco, José Maria da Silva Paranhos Jr., who served as foreign minister from 1902 to 1912. Under his leadership, many of the nation's outstanding border disputes were settled, and Brazil became an active participant in multilateral diplomacy.

Politics under the Old Republic

Two prominent military figures were chosen in an indirect election to become the first leaders of the republic. Deodoro da Fonseca, the leader of the coup, became president, and Floriano Peixoto, the leader of the traditionalists, was elected vice president. After da Fonseca resigned in November 1891, Peixoto succeeded him as president. Thereafter, the presidents of the republic—with one exception—were all civilians. The dominant political organization was in theory a national Republican Party. But that party was little more than a regional collection of state notables. Many of them had been involved in the old republican movement, but many had also been sympathetic to the monarchy.

Serious challenges faced the new government. In 1893 it was forced to confront the "rebellion in the backlands," which stemmed from the decision by a seminomadic holy man known as Antonio Conselheiro to establish a settlement in the backlands of the northeastern state of Bahia. Conselheiro favored the restoration of the monarchy and condemned republicans as atheists and Masons. The state governor unwisely decided to challenge and eliminate Canudos, the fanatics' base. When this military expedition failed, the state government called on Rio de Janeiro to support its efforts. Several federal interventions were turned back or defeated until the village was destroyed in 1897. The episode generated widespread international press attention as well as a good deal of soul searching within the Brazilian intellectual elite. Many cited the incident as an indication that Brazil remained suspended between two futures—one as a civilized country and the other as a barbaric society.[12]

The first decade of the new republic was also disturbed by the appearance of a group known as Jacobins, principally in Rio de Janeiro. The movement, which favored a strong republic and deeply opposed any monarchist sentiment, was made up of members of the lower middle class, laborers, and low-ranked military personnel, who were hurt by inflation and a drop in living standards in the early 1890s. The movement died out by the end of the century, but Jacobin-like movements continued to come and go. Poverty and marginalization were a way of life, not just for former slaves but also for a large segment of the population outside the major cities as well as in the growing slum areas that began to circle the major urban centers.

Along with poverty and unrest, regional issues remained a constant challenge for the republic. A recurrent source of problems was the continuing search for autonomy by the southern state of Rio Grande do Sul. Demographically and economically different from the rest of the federation—slavery was not an issue in the province; the affinity with Argentina and Uruguay was far stronger than the affinity with the northeast; the region was an important and diversified agricultural producer—it had become an increasingly important player in the last decades of the empire. The state's elite was deeply divided, often violently so, between the traditionalists along the Uruguayan border and the republicans, mostly newcomers located along the coast and in the mountains. These disputes often spilled onto the national political stage.

Nonetheless, by the turn of the century, state rivalries had been more or less balanced within a broad republican federation. The coffee oligarchy in São Paulo enjoyed national political and economic power, despite an uneasy relationship with the remainder of the country. The political system settled into a relatively stable process in which the poorer states generally supported the Paulistas' legislative priorities, especially where coffee was concerned. In return, except when law and order were seriously threatened, state governors and elites were given autonomy to rule largely as they saw fit. The presidency rotated among leaders from São Paulo and Minas Gerais, and most national political offices were held by representatives from those two states and from Rio Grande do Sul. These three major states pursued their own interests, intersecting in Rio de Janeiro as needed. The other states were basically left alone.

Critically, no institution was capable of unifying the country and identifying national development goals. There was no truly national Republican Party; instead, each state organized its own party to represent the interests of the local elite. These local parties negotiated support from potential dissidents and loyalists by rewarding them through clientelist and patrimonial arrangements. In the most backward parts of the north and northeast, the local "colonels"—landowners who were descendants of the leaders of the nineteenth-century national guard—delivered the vote at election time, but they, too, had to make their peace with the national government to guarantee ongoing support for their political position. In the more advanced states, the local Republican Party became part of an efficient and well-oiled bureaucratic structure of patronage.

In theory, the voters could have held their political leaders accountable to a higher standard, but the average Brazilian showed little interest in doing so. Turnout at election time was very low, although it increased marginally over time. Voting was not secret, electoral fraud was widespread, and few local political officials respected the electoral records. Lawlessness and the potential for conflict were constant features of political life.

Forces of Change

Despite the stasis at the institutional and political levels, important demographic and social changes were under way. Almost 4 million immigrants entered Brazil over the period of a century, from independence to 1930. The vast majority settled in the center-south and south of the country. São Paulo was the largest recipient. The immigrant flow was not dominated by any one nationality. Overall Italians were the largest group, but significant numbers of Portuguese, Spaniards, Japanese, Syrians, and Lebanese also found a new home in Brazil. With the arrival of new settlers with old-world skills, agricultural production began to increase to meet new demand in the growing cities.

However, little industrialization took place. As Werner Baer notes, booming coffee exports continued to lead the economy, while the industrial sector—which was dominated by textiles—lagged.[13] The two trends have often been linked. The success of coffee probably crowded out other forms of investment, while a coffee aristocracy little interested in innovation may have devalued entrepreneurship and competition. Lack of investment in physical infrastructure may have contributed to slow industrialization. Monetary and exchange rate policies probably played a role. And the emphasis in higher education on law and medicine, and not mathematics, physics, and engineering, was part of the mix.

The End of the Republic

The final decade of the old republic saw growing political turmoil, coupled with increasing concern within the military about the future of the republic. In July 1922 a dramatic break with the military hierarchy occurred when the famous lieutenants' movement broke out with a revolt at Fort Copacabana in Rio de Janeiro. While the rebellion was repressed by the government, the young officers became national symbols of disgust with corruption and the "business as usual" politics of the 1920s. Other rebellions took place, notably in São Paulo in 1924. A variety of opposition groups joined forces under the political leadership of Luis Carlos Prestes. The Prestes column left the southeast and moved across the northeast attempting to build a social protest movement, but the local colonels and their hired guns were able to maintain the status quo in the backlands. The column crossed into Bolivia in exile in 1927, but the pressure for change continued to build. Former minister of finance Getúlio Vargas spearheaded a move to expand the role of Rio Grande do Sul in national politics. And a new political organization, the Democratic Party, was created in São Paulo with a liberal program that demanded political reform.

Seeking to keep power in the hands of the coffee oligarchy, Brazil's president, Washington Luis, nominated a fellow Paulista as his successor. The leaders of Minas Gerais and Rio Grande do Sul reacted immediately. They formed an anti–São Paulo coalition—the Liberal Alliance—and offered Getúlio Vargas the presidential nomination. In the middle of the campaign, the 1929 financial crisis occurred. Financial panic swept across the Brazilian economy.

Julio Prestes, a member of the traditional oligarchy in São Paulo, won the presidential election on March 1, 1930. It appeared as though the oligarchy was safe. But on July 26, 1930, Vargas's running mate, João Pessoa, was murdered in the northeastern city of Recife. He became a martyr for the revolutionary cause. Within the younger military officer corps, rumblings began. An antiregime movement quickly emerged across the country. To preclude bloodshed, the senior military command in Rio de Janeiro deposed Washington Luis on October 24, 1930. Vargas arrived in Rio de Janeiro from Rio Grande do Sul and took power on November 3. The old republic was dead. The post-1889 oligarchies were marginalized. A new generation of younger military officers, politicians, bureaucrats, and businessmen took charge. But the future remained unclear: What did Vargas and his revolution represent for Brazil? Would the country become less dependent on coffee revenues? What were the alternatives? Did the new government have new answers to old social problems? Were the distant state and regional tensions of the northeast amenable to political reconciliation? As Washington Luis followed the emperor into exile in Europe, Vargas and his gaucho backers assembled in Rio de Janeiro to address these hitherto intractable questions.

The Making of Modern Brazil, 1930–64

The significance of 1930 cannot be overestimated. For the first time since the founding of Brazil, the agrarian aristocracy lost its grip on power and would never regain its previous preeminence in national affairs. In addition, 1930 marked the beginning of a long and tortured process of modernization and industrialization. These changes did not pass unchallenged. The traditional oligarchs fought to preserve their influence and autonomy. Nonetheless, by the middle of the 1930s, Getúlio Vargas was the dominant, if not the only, power broker in Brazil.

The Arrival of Getúlio Vargas

Few, if any, political characters are more controversial in Brazilian history than Getúlio Vargas, who governed Brazil in different guises for eighteen years: as provisional president from 1930 to 1934, as the indirectly elected chief executive from 1934 to 1937, as a "soft" dictator from 1937 to 1945, and as the directly elected president from 1951 until his suicide in 1954. As the political representative of the outrider state of Rio Grande do Sul, Vargas initially spoke for change. His first and perhaps most important initiative was to centralize political and administrative power in the capital. Immediately upon taking power, the provisional government removed all of the state governors (with the exception of the governor of Minas Gerais, who was considered an ally) and appointed *interventors* in their place. These officials, who were charged with carrying out policies decided in Rio de Janeiro, were chosen from among the president's close allies and the younger military officials who had helped bring him to power.

Vargas moved quickly to consolidate his position and deal with potential competitors, including the "lieutenants" who had helped to bring about the end of the Old Republic. This group included different factions, some wholly supportive of the central government, others committed to a different and often more radical reform agenda. Vargas and his staff were assiduous in neutralizing the more aggressive lieutenants, and by the mid-1930s the movement had fragmented. Many joined the regime; others moved either left or right on the national and regional political spectrum.

Vargas also sought to ensure the support of two important social groups: urban workers and the new middle class. In November 1930 he created Brazil's first Ministry of Labor, Industry, and Commerce as an intermediary between labor and the state. An important goal of the new ministry was to augment the government's influence over the urban labor force. Only those unions recognized by the Ministry of Labor were considered legal, and the labor leadership was chosen by the state. The ministry also instated the *imposto sindical*—compulsory annual union dues equivalent to one day's wages—and the collected funds were then distributed to the government-recognized unions. At the same time, independent unions were forbidden in the cities, all labor organization was outlawed in the countryside, and labor linkages to political parties were forbidden. The state incorporation of labor allowed Vargas to turn potential political opponents into clients and would ultimately have far-reaching consequences for Brazil's economic and industrial development as well as its political future.[1]

At the same time, a second new ministry—the Ministry of Education and Health—was established to serve the urban middle class. Isolated for decades between the oligarchy and the urban proletariat, these were the wage earners, the professionals, the mid-level bureaucrats.[2] Vargas understood the political potential of harnessing their dreams and expectations to the new regime. The new ministry was intended to bolster their loyalty by creating a modern system of education and training, from the top down. As part of this drive, Brazil's first university was opened in 1934 in São Paulo, followed a year later by the launch of a university in the Federal District. One goal of these initiatives was to create a new cadre of talent for public administration. Another was to open up professional opportunities for members of the middle class, who feared "falling" into the lower classes. Through education, the middle class could seek and protect a superior position in the social hierarchy.

In addition to appealing to urban workers and the middle class, Vargas reached out to the Roman Catholic Church. In April 1931 the government authorized religious teaching in the country's public schools; in October the giant statue of Christ was raised over the city on Corcovado Mountain in the center of Rio de Janeiro. The Catholic hierarchy quickly became firm supporters of the new order.

These moves were driven as much by political necessity as by a desire to transform Brazil. The traditional oligarchs remained influential even though they had lost national political power. They dominated many of the traditional institutions of the state, and they were ferociously opposed to the new order. This opposition was strongest in the state of São Paulo, where the coffee oligarchy wanted little to do with the upstart government. Various *interventors* were sent to São Paulo; all failed to administer national policy. Finally, in a desperate act of defiance, the state rebelled against the national government on July 9, 1932, with the tacit support of dissident groups within the Rio Grande do Sul political hierarchy. The battle was waged as one for liberal democracy and autonomy. But Vargas was able to quarantine the military conflict in São Paulo. The odds were overwhelmingly against the Paulistas, who surrendered in October 1932. As neither side wanted to continue the conflict, steps were taken to pacify the political ambitions of the state; in turn the Paulista elites accepted the new national government.

Once the conflict with São Paulo had been resolved, the government was able to turn to the challenge of reframing the country's political institutions. In this area, Vargas showed himself to be an astute and formidable politician. Early in his administration he remained vague as to the ultimate institutional structure he preferred. Bowing graciously to pressures for normalizing the country's political status, he agreed to elections in May 1933 for a national constituent assembly. The body, under his direction, quickly drafted a new constitution that was promulgated in July 1934—the new constitution established a four-year presidential term with no possibility for reelection.[3] Vargas took the oath of office a day later for a presidential term that would end in May 1938.

Turmoil Abroad and at Home

The Vargas regime had seized power in the context of world turmoil. The global economy had collapsed in 1929. The new government, bound to coffee as its principal foreign exchange earner, was faced with a sharp drop in demand worldwide. Coffee policy was moved from São Paulo and concentrated in the capital. It was decided that the government would buy excess crops and destroy part of the harvest in order to reduce the supply and maintain its price. This remained government policy until the end of the Vargas era. More broadly, the 1930s were, as for all of the countries in the region, difficult. Brazil was frequently on the brink of economic and financial crisis. The state of the government's finances was dire, and in September 1931 it suspended payments on its foreign debt.

Vargas had also come to power in an increasingly polarized and ideological world order. A series of authoritarian, neo-populist governments had reached power in Europe beginning with Mussolini in Italy in 1922, Salazar in Portugal in 1932, and Hitler in Germany in 1933; a succession of right-wing, repressive regimes would also emerge in Central Europe as the 1930s progressed. The antithesis of these regimes in ideological terms was the communist government that had transformed Russia into the Soviet Union following the 1917 revolution. Liberal democracy in the 1930s was a challenged "brand."

The same political currents were manifest in Brazil in the 1930s. In 1932 the fascist movement took form as the Brazilian Integralist Movement (AIB), which trumpeted its values as "God, Fatherland, and Family." A few years later, a communist-inspired umbrella movement of the left appeared in the form of the National Liberal Alliance (ANL), which went public in March 1935. While the AIB generally supported the regime, the ANL called for its overthrow, by violence if necessary. Threatened by the growth in support for both groups, the government closed the AIB in July 1935. Its leadership went underground and launched a coup d'état in November. The effort failed quickly as loyal government troops neutralized the AIB forces. The aftermath was predictable: the regime's security forces used the revolt as an excuse for repression, and the authoritarian streak within the governing coalition deepened. Vargas, as usual, stood back, quietly observing and tacitly condoning the confirmation of his presidential powers.

Against this backdrop, preparations began for the presidential election in January 1938. With Vargas presumably unable to stand for a second term, candidates from across the political spectrum began campaigning. But as many suspected, the Vargas forces were not about to yield power. A communist plot was "discovered" in late 1937. Congress declared a state of war and suspended all constitutional guarantees. Within days, Brazil's brief experiment with representative government ended. On November 15, 1937, Vargas announced the formation of the so-called new state (*estado novo*). There was little opposition to this move. The liberal governor of São Paulo called on the armed forces to resist the putsch; they declined to do so. The AIB revolted in May 1938, following an unsuccessful effort by its leader Plínio Salgado to collaborate with the Vargas regime; it was quickly defeated. Given deteriorating world conditions and the fear of a possible civil war at home, key political actors quickly endorsed the new state. That endorsement would last through World War II.

Estado Novo: The New State

The new state was in many ways the culmination of the trends that had begun in 1930. State centralization deepened. Liberal democracy and its advocates were silenced. The nonpolitical "educational and professional" vocation of middle-class Brazil received high priority. Industrialization continued, and the new bourgeoisie pushed for state intervention in support of their expansion plans. These efforts often benefited from the support of the military. For example, to satisfy both the armed forces' drive for autonomy in arms production and the growing need in the industrial sector for a steady supply of steel, the government made the construction of Latin America's first steel mill, located in Volta Redonda in the state of Minas Gerais, a national priority. Completed in 1946, the project was financed with assistance from the United States, which was grateful for Brazil's diplomatic and military support. After a brief dalliance with the Axis powers in the mid-1930s, driven mostly by reasons related to trade, the Vargas regime declared war on Germany and Italy in 1942. Two years later, the government sent Brazilian troops to Europe to fight alongside the Allied forces. The Brazilian Expeditionary Force would become a source of national pride and, ultimately, of political influence in internal affairs following the war.

In addition to steel, petroleum became an important focus of government policy. Domestic production was insignificant. Consequently, beginning in 1938 national policy began to consider alternatives in the energy field. In 1938 a decree-law nationalized the refining of both foreign and Brazilian oil. This decree opened a long-running national debate over the control of the petroleum sector that would only end with the creation of Petrobras, the state-owned oil monopoly, in October 1953.

In the social field, the government undertook further efforts to neutralize possible labor militancy. A final codification of labor legislation took place in 1943. The new legislation was comprehensive—it provided retirement and pension plans, a minimum wage, a work week limited to forty-eight hours, paid annual vacation leave, maternal benefits and child care, educational facilities, training programs and literacy campaigns, safety and health standards in the workplace, and job security.[4] Other measures were taken to allow the Ministry of Labor and its courts, spies, and judges to monitor and control the labor movement. As the federal bureaucracy expanded, the number of nonpolitical professional positions grew, and the middle class withdrew into a focus on work and home, with little ambition to be active politically. Finally, Vargas added "father of the poor" to his many other roles in order to consolidate his support among the urban masses. The government's propagandists successfully used such policies to burnish the image of Vargas as the father of modern Brazil.

"Modern" was a relative term. As Lincoln Gordon writes, "Almost 70 percent of the population still lived in rural areas in 1940, two-thirds of the adults were illiterate, and the rudimentary conditions of communications and transport left large regions in isolation."[5] Brazil was a "classic case of incomplete transformation from traditional stasis to modern economic growth."[6] While incipient industrialization had been under way for a few decades in São Paulo, the old Brazil remained agrarian and traditional. The agricultural sector was the largest contributor to GDP. Coffee remained the dominant export crop and the critical foreign exchange earner. Commercial agriculture produced smaller crops of sugar, cotton, tobacco, and cacao for export, but these were relatively minor in the overall profile of exports.

As the 1940s opened, there was little dissent over the internal political order. But as the Allied victory in World War II grew increasingly likely, a debate began over the relationship between Brazil's dictatorship at home and its support for an overseas war to defeat fascism and restore democracy. Civil society began to mobilize hesitantly and to test the political waters. In 1937 university students organized the National Student Union during the first National Student Congress. The organization was established to participate actively in the social struggles of the time and in the

1940s played an important role in fighting to end the *estado novo,* taking a strict position against Vargas in student congresses and organized protests (such as the March of Silence against the Vargas government in 1943).[7] The government issued a vague offer to consider holding elections after the end of the war. Key members of the Vargas regime began to express doubts about its future. Sensing a change in the political mood, the press began to ignore state censorship.

Vargas understood the situation. In February 1945 a process was put in place to create a new electoral code. A direct presidential election and the election of delegates for a new constituent assembly were scheduled in December 1945. State elections were decreed for May 1946. For the first time in Brazilian history, political parties organized. A conservative group on the center-right, the National Democratic Union (UDN), represented the old liberal opposition and the traditional foes of the *estado novo*. Vargas, astutely, decided to build on his dual sources of political strength. He ratified the creation of the Social Democratic Party (PSD), which represented the essential elements of the state apparatus. As an insurance policy, he also oversaw the establishment of a small Brazilian Labor Party; its purpose was to capture the vote and support of the growing labor movement. The fourth important party was the traditional Communist Party of Brazil (PCB).

Midway through 1945, the apparently quiescent Vargas machine came alive with a nationwide campaign calling for the president to stay. Two important missteps on the part of the Vargas administration led the armed forces to confront the president and demand his resignation. The first was issuing a decree to move up the date for state and local elections to the same day as the national elections (December 2), which meant that incumbent government officials who wished to stand for governorships would have to resign thirty days before the elections, leaving the president with room to fill the government with his supporters. The second was a move to replace the chief of police of Rio de Janeiro (João Alberto) with the president's brother (Benjamin Vargas). This move was opposed by Góes Monteiro, the minister of war, who held a standing agreement with Alberto that they both would resign at the same time.[8] Like his imperial and civilian predecessors, Vargas accepted the decision of the military and retired to his ranch in Rio Grande do Sul. Once again, the armed forces used their "moderating power" to introduce regime change, and, once again, the central figure in the old regime understood the rules of the game and left peacefully.[9] The center held, and Brazil moved forward.

The 1946 Republic

The departure of Getúlio Vargas, after fifteen years of personalist rule, represented a critical juncture in Brazilian history. Many observers expected or hoped that the old Brazil of slavery, empire, *café com leite*, and authoritarian rule would yield to a new, but untried, civilian, modern political system—"an experiment in democracy," as Thomas Skidmore termed it.[10] But instead the combination of inexperience with democracy, poor economic decisions, the failure to address the rising expectations of the middle class, and the return of Brazil's northeast as a political problem after a century of neglect, resulted in the dramatic and tragic collapse of the democratic experiment in 1964.

The Transition to Democracy

The daunting odds facing the democratic experiment were suggested by the December 1945 presidential election, which looked more to the past than to the future. General Eurico Gaspar Dutra ran as the PSD candidate; he had been a key player and insider in national politics since 1930. The UDN, which was to remain in opposition for almost the entire duration of the 1946 republic, put forward Brigadier Eduardo Gomes as its candidate. Gomes was a hero of the 1922 lieutenants' revolt in Copacabana and a long-standing critic of the Vargas regime. Gomes initially appeared poised to win, but Dutra and the PSD machine turned out the vote in the large states and took 55 percent of the vote. Gomes did best in the underdeveloped areas of the country and received 35 percent of the vote. The Communist Party of Brazil, to the surprise of many, placed third, with 10 percent of the votes cast. It was a momentary victory. In the context of the cold war, the party was forced underground soon after. Congress approved legislation to cancel the mandate of all PCB public officials and those in positions of leadership in the unions.

Elections were also held for the Chamber of Deputies and the Senate, which were to serve as a constituent assembly to draft a new constitution. The PSD won absolute majorities in both houses. Dutra took office early in 1946; the constitution was completed at the end of the year. While democratic in form, it remained corporatist in content. For example, the right to strike was guaranteed by the constitution, but the Congress approved a law that defined which activities were "essential" for the economy and where strikes were not permitted; this included almost every field of economic activity. The union tax, a main source of support for union bosses aligned with the government, was retained. Many similar measures that were redolent of the *estado novo* were incorporated with little, if any, opposition.

The Dutra government was predictably conservative in political terms. The cancellation of the rights of the PCB clearly indicated the government's ideological position, as did its support for the United States. Similarly, on the economic front, the government hewed to the policies of the past, sometimes with disastrous results. The country's wartime foreign exchange reserves disappeared quickly in an import spree. The balance of payments emerged as a perennial problem, and exchange rate controls were imposed from 1947 until 1953. Throughout this period, Brazil's currency, the cruzeiro, remained overvalued, which favored traditional agricultural interests over the industrial class that was emerging in the south. The overvaluation also led the government to resort to a system of import licensing to keep demand for foreign goods under control. The licensing process became highly political and corrupt, damaging the government's credibility.

During this period, Brazilian leaders became increasingly pessimistic about the country's economic future. The key concern was Brazil's reliance on exports of primary products. With an overvalued currency, the terms of trade after the war did not favor exports of such products; in addition, long-term prospects for commodity prices were gloomy, while Brazil steadily lost global market share to its competitors abroad.[11] Prompted by the writings of economists like Raul Prebisch at the United Nations Economic Commission for Latin America and the Caribbean (ECLAC) in Santiago, Chile, policymakers began to show growing interest in the policy of import substitution industrialization. However, efforts at longer-term planning in the Dutra years failed. It would take the return of Vargas to power to commit the country firmly to import substitution industrialization.

While in political exile in Rio Grande do Sul, Vargas remained popular with many Brazilian citizens. He was elected federal deputy and senator from several states but chose not to take an active role in the early years of the republic. But it was clear to most observers that he had not abdicated national power but had instead put a "hold" on its use until the right circumstances provided the moment to return to national life. That moment arrived in 1950. For the October 1950 presidential election, Vargas cobbled together a coalition including leaders from the Social Democratic Party, the Labor Party, and the Progressive Social Party, a new group founded by Adhemar de Barros, the charismatic populist who had been elected governor of São Paulo with communist support in 1947. The endorsement of de Barros helped Vargas to defeat Eduardo Gomes, again the center-right UDN candidate, by a wide margin and to take the oath of office as Brazil's president in January 1951.

The Fourth Act

Vargas remained a controversial and polarizing figure. During the campaign, he ran on a platform of support for industrialization and the working class, to the alarm of many in the middle class and traditional elites. Once back in power, he actively supported the import substitution industrialization model. In 1952 he created the National Bank of Economic and Social Development to support state-led industrialization. The government also invested directly in key sectors, such as energy. In 1953 Vargas nationalized the petroleum sector and created the state oil enterprise Petrobras. Such bold measures frightened the middle class and conservatives who linked the radicalization of public policy to the rise of new, aggressive urban political leaders. In addition, opposition to the regime was fueled by its inability to control inflation, which returned in the early 1950s. Vargas changed ministers several times in an effort to address the growing tension caused by inflation, but to no avail.

As well as alienating the middle class, Vargas's economic policies helped to deepen the divide within Brazil's armed forces over internal politics, strategies of economic development, and the appropriate role of Brazil in world affairs. On one side, the nationalists were strong supporters of industrialization with a key role for the government as regulator and investor in important areas of the economy, such as petroleum, communications, and transportation. They were suspicious of direct foreign investment as a potential threat to national sovereignty. On the other side of the divide, the *entreguistas* (sell-outs) favored a more moderate role for the state.[12] While not favoring a takeover of the economy by foreign investors, they saw the merit of investment to bring new technology and know-how to Brazil. In foreign affairs, the nationalists were highly suspicious of the United States and looked to distance Brazil from Washington; their opponents saw America as a key ally in the fight against international communism.

Getúlio Vargas appeared to play increasingly to the nationalists and to his populist base. His criticism of foreign capital grew fierce. On May Day 1954 he infuriated conservatives by announcing a 100 percent increase in the minimum wage. The opposition National Democratic Union stepped up its attacks on the regime, contributing further to political polarization. That summer, some of Vargas's closest political advisers decided to strike at the opposition by eliminating one of its key spokesmen, a charismatic journalist named Carlos Lacerda.

In early August 1954 an assassination attempt was made. Lacerda escaped serious injury, but a young air force officer was killed. This event galvanized the various factions that opposed Vargas. On August 23 a group of high-ranking military officers called for the president's resignation. Depressed and isolated, Vargas committed suicide in the presidential palace the following day. He left an emotional letter, blaming his death on national and international conspirators who sought to overturn his progressive policies. Popular protests, with strong participation of the Communist Party of Brazil, broke out in the major urban centers. While the military maintained order, the future was unclear.

To maintain legality, always important to the armed forces, the vice president, João Café Filho, was allowed to assume the presidency. A conservative who had been elected independently of Vargas, he formed a cabinet with a UDN majority and affirmed that the elections already scheduled for October 1955 would take place. In the uneasy environment created by Vargas's suicide, the parties chose their candidates. The Social Democratic Party selected Juscelino Kubitschek, the young and dynamic governor of Minas Gerais, who also received the endorsement of the Labor Party. The UDN chose a senior military officer, General Juarez Távora, whose campaign focused on the need for morality in public life. In contrast, Kubitschek called for modernization and rapid economic growth. He won with 36 percent of the vote. Running separately, João Goulart (known as Jango), a Vargas protégé and former labor minister who had become a lightning rod for the conservative opposition, was elected vice president with strong support from urban labor and nationalists.

Between the election and the inauguration in January 1956, a series of events demonstrated how unpredictable national politics were and would remain. President Café Filho stepped down due to health problems. His successor, the president of the Chamber of Deputies, was suspected of supporting the conservative forces that wanted to prevent Kubitschek and Jango from taking office. He was deposed and succeeded by the president of the Senate. President Café Filho, in better health, tried to reassume his office. Congress demurred and confirmed the Senate president, who finally transferred power to Kubitschek in early 1956.

Juscelino Kubitschek and Developmentalism

Kubitschek pledged that Brazil would develop fifty years during his five-year term. And he did in fact oversee significant economic and social change, as well as the building of a new capital city, Brasília, in less than four years. Industrialization, which had been gathering speed in the first half of the decade, accelerated. With the deepening of import substitution industrialization, Brazil's export profile moved away from coffee and agricultural products and to industrial goods and more sophisticated raw materials. Industrial progress also resulted in high rates of economic growth. The average yearly real growth rate from 1947 to 1952 was more than 6 percent, and in the intensive years of the Kubitschek government, the growth rate reached 7.8 percent. As Lincoln Gordon writes, "That expansion was not merely quantitative; it moved from light industry into increasingly sophisticated consumer durable goods, intermediate goods, and a wide range of capital goods. With industrialization came more than a doubling of urbanization."[13]

Brazil also achieved some measure of social progress. Life expectancy rose, infant mortality fell, and adult literacy improved. But inflation continued to put pressure on the living standards of most Brazilians. Together, these developments contributed to a flowering of what today would be called "civil society," the emergence of a new generation of civilian elites, and the growing radicalization of national politics.

The changing role of the Roman Catholic Church both reflected and contributed to these trends. Long a strong supporter of the status quo, the church in the mid-1950s became a leader in the fight against social inequity. This change was spearheaded by Archbishop Hélder Câmara, who oversaw the creation of the National Council of Brazilian Bishops in 1955. Over the next five to six years, he was instrumental in winning Vatican approval for a new generation of young, modernizing bishops, primarily in Brazil's underdeveloped northeast. The council worked closely with the Kubitschek government to raise the profile of the northeast at the national level. One of its most important accomplishments was the passage of legislation that established the Superintendence for the Development of the Northeast (SUDENE) in 1959. SUDENE was created over the opposition of local political elites, who were threatened by the idea of modernization. Not one deputy from the region voted for the new federal agency, which was led by a young ECLAC-trained economist, Celso Furtado. As superintendent, Furtado walked a fine line between his mandate to restructure economic and social forces in the region and the realities of political power, which remained, for the most part, in the hands of the local colonels and the most conservative political organizations in the country.

The Roman Catholic Church also signed an agreement with Jânio Quadros, who succeeded Kubitschek as president in 1961, to coordinate a series of radio schools and literacy programs in the northeast. The goal of this initiative was to challenge poverty and marginalization in an often overlooked region. But it was viewed by the traditional elites as a threat to their control, especially when church workers moved into the countryside in an effort to raise the political consciousness of the peasants. These efforts were seen as subversive in the early 1960s, particularly after the success of the Cuban Revolution in 1959 and Fidel Castro's subsequent efforts to export his revolution to South America.

Independent of the church's efforts, a young lawyer and political activist, Francisco Julião, supported the organization of local peasant leagues in the northeast. The leagues, which had begun to challenge the distribution of land rights in the 1950s, soon came to represent peasant resistance against centuries of repression and neglect. The U.S. government became increasingly alarmed at this pattern of radicalization, and the Kennedy administration decided to support a major foreign aid effort to neutralize the radical activists.[14]

While the northeast began to stir and then ferment, in the south a parallel intellectual debate got under way, launched by the formation of the Higher Institute of Brazilian Studies within the Ministry of Education in Rio de Janeiro. What began as an intellectual and theoretical inquiry into the future of Brazil grew into an increasingly contentious argument among intellectuals, student activists, journalists, and politicians over the capitalist model of development, the role of traditional institutions in Brazil, and the appropriate model for resolving the glaring inequalities in Brazilian society. Catholic lay groups were very much involved in this debate, which by the end of the decade took on an increasingly ideological tone.[15]

Increasing divisiveness also characterized the political party system, which splintered over the course of the 1950s. Beginning with three parties in 1946 (four including the proscribed Communist Party), Brazil had thirteen parties by 1964. While many of the new parties were small and represented specific interest groups or lobbies, their proliferation caused stalemates in the national and state legislatures as well as increasing tension between the executive and the Congress.

Jânio Quadros and the Beginning of the End

The confluence of new ideas, new social movements, and new political parties provided the backdrop for the 1960 presidential election. The candidate of the government forces was General Henrique Lott, a former defense minister and representative of the "legalist" wing of the armed forces. The National Democratic Union's candidate was Jânio Quadros, the governor of São Paulo, who used his usual symbol of a kitchen broom to indicate that he would sweep away all that was wrong in Brazilian political life. For the first time in the history of the 1946 republic, the UDN candidate won, and João Goulart was reelected vice president.

Quadros took office in early 1961; he resigned and abandoned Brasília in August of the same year. In that short span of time, he managed to alienate most of the leading players in national politics during his failed attempts to expand executive powers and enact political reforms and economic measures to counter inflation. Quadros also alienated Brazilian foreign policy moderates with a so-called independent stance favoring closer ties with the Soviet bloc and Cuba and distancing Brazil from the United States.[16] His abrupt resignation created an institutional crisis that signaled the beginning of the end of the constitutional order. Vice President Goulart (Jango), the *bête noire* of the conservative forces in national politics, was on a visit to communist China at the time of the succession crisis. As he prepared to return to Brasília to assume office, the armed forces divided. The conservative wing refused to allow him to return or to take the oath of office. A nationalist wing supported by his brother-in-law, Leonel Brizola, governor of the state of Rio Grande do Sul, argued that Jango was Quadros's legitimate heir. The stand-off finally ended in compromise: Jango could return, but only after the constitution had been amended to establish a parliamentary regime that would allow him to serve essentially as a figurehead chief of state. He was sworn in on September 7, 1961.

Jango and the Road to Revolution

Jango did not create the crisis atmosphere in which he assumed power, but he appeared to do all he could to exacerbate the situation during his short period in power. A hesitant, often shy politician, he appeared easily swayed by his brother-in-law and by a medley of advisers who often seemed more interested in creating crises than in managing or resolving them.

On all fronts—economic, social, and political—Jango inherited a tired, frightened, and troubled Brazil. Economically, the bloom was off the rose of import substitution industrialization. As a result of borrowing undertaken to finance import-substituting investment, the country was deeply indebted by 1961, and balance-of-payments problems loomed, partly because in the rush to deepen import substitution industrialization, preceding governments had overlooked or forgotten the need to promote and diversify exports. The Goulart administration faced mounting pressure to service the national debt (much of it short term), allow profit remittances by foreign firms, and attract foreign capital. In addition, while industry had grown smartly in the 1950s, agriculture had been neglected. As urban migration increased, food supplies became tighter, and prices rose. There was growing concern that urban food shortages might become a reality and that the rising price of food would exacerbate inflationary pressures and social tension.

Industrial growth had also resulted in deepening inequality, creating deep gaps in different regional, sectoral, and income groups. Many people looked to the government to educate the poor and integrate them into the "new" Brazil. But the national education system had long been neglected, which created obstacles not only to social integration but also to further industrial growth. Similarly, the country's physical infrastructure had been allowed to deteriorate, hindering economic, social, and political integration.

Politically, several trends favored disaster. Coalitions formed at the state and national level to win elections, but then fell apart, making it impossible to govern. Politicians changed party labels with impunity. Legislative debates in Brasília became increasingly illogical and unproductive. The radicalization of urban student and political groups continued, with many engaging in Marxist-influenced rhetoric. Meanwhile, the middle class, which after being betrayed by Vargas and overlooked by Kubitschek had dreamed of salvation at the hands of the center-right government of Quadros, once again expected the worst from Goulart.[17] As they hunkered down to await what they saw as the inevitable collapse of the regime, they turned away from politics and retreated into a focus on work and family.

As expected, Goulart and his team pushed a nationalist-populist agenda. The government supported land reform and legislation to allow illiterates and enlisted men in the armed services to vote, all measures that smelled of socialism or communism to the traditional elite. In addition, the administration favored a far greater role for the state in the economy. Proposals to nationalize a wide range of economic activities were popular. Limitations on the remittance of profits abroad by foreign

firms received widespread popular support as the government intensified its anticapitalist rhetoric.

The government was able to rely on the support of several political
groups, including a new group within the UDN, the so-called *bossa nova;*
a more radical "compact group" within the Labor Party; the energized
PCB (still formally illegal); and a new union movement that rejected the
Vargas-era controls and sought independence from the central government. The actions of these allies frequently further alienated the opposition. Growing labor militancy, for example, led to the creation of the
Workers General Staff in 1962, a labor organization that agitated in
favor of labor-oriented reforms.[18] Strike activity became an increasingly
popular method of putting pressure on Brasília, frightening the business
and commercial elites and the middle class. And in 1963 Goulart abandoned one of the major compromises of the Vargas era by signing legislation to legalize rural unionization. The law opened a new front in the
confrontation between the traditional landlords and their backers and
the nationalists and opened the door to a fight to organize and politicize
the once quiet countryside.

Goulart also sought to get the economy back on track by appointing
two distinguished members of the political class to prepare a new Three-
Year Plan (*Plano Trienal*). Celso Furtado was called from Recife and
joined forces with former foreign minister San Thiago Dantas to reorganize the national economy. But the effort came to naught. By the summer
of 1963 it was clear there was no political appetite in Brasília for the drastic policy innovations that would be required to "fix" the economy, and
Furtado and Dantas were dismissed.

Meanwhile, signs of political trouble were multiplying. State elections
were held in October 1962, and while the moderates did well, two victo-
ries put the conservatives on alert. The first was Leonel Brizola's election
by a huge margin to the federal Congress as a representative of Rio de
Janeiro. Brizola, who was married to Goulart's sister, was widely seen as
the Svengali of the Goulart regime.[19] The second was the election of
Miguel Arraes as governor of the state of Pernambuco, the center of the
peasant league revolt. Arraes was seen as the leading leftist in the northeast and a strong supporter of rural unions, the peasant leagues, popular
culture, and other initiatives that openly challenged the status quo.

In addition, it was clear that the parliamentary compromise of September 1961, which significantly limited the president's powers, chafed
at the Goulart forces, which began a campaign to move up the date of a

plebiscite to restore presidential powers. The vote was held in January 1963, and the Brazilian people overwhelmingly approved the restoration of Goulart's presidential powers.

These moves increased the disquiet within the conservative wing of the military, which viewed the polarization and radicalization under way as a growing challenge to the military institution and a democratic Brazil.[20] Several military-supported institutions quietly debated options if the need to take action occurred. The Superior War College, organized in 1949 with the assistance of the United States, had for many years studied different national trajectories for the country, working in concert with targeted allies in the private sector and the government. In addition, several "institutes" had opened in the early 1960s, some supported by the U.S. Central Intelligence Agency, to prepare for an eventual confrontation with the left.

Conservative members of the military had further cause for concern when a serious rebellion broke out among noncommissioned officers in the navy and air force in September 1963. The immediate cause was a decision by the Supreme Court that rejected efforts to give them the right to vote. While the rebellion was suppressed, it again raised the issue of a threat to the military command structure.

One month later, the Congress rejected draft legislation that would have authorized the expropriation of rural landholdings without compensation. The reaction of the nationalist left was that forced occupation and distribution might be the only alternative to move the radical reform process forward. The president requested authority from Congress to declare a thirty-day state of siege to maintain order, especially in the countryside; his request was denied. There was growing suspicion among moderates and centrists that the government's goal was to force through its reforms with or without democratic legal and institutional procedures.

For old hands at Brazilian politics, it was fairly obvious that the regime in power in January 1964 would not be there by the end of the year. Either the Goulart forces would take command and eliminate even the façade of republican government or the military would take action to neutralize the presidential palace and its radical reform agenda. Soon Goulart and his closest advisers decided that it was time to make their move to "liberate" the country. Plans were made for a series of public rallies to mobilize public opinion and intimidate the opposition into allowing the government to rule by decree.

The opening salvo was a massive rally in Rio de Janeiro on March 13, 1964. The grandees of the regime took to the stage in front of a vast sea of enthusiastic supporters. Banners called for the legalization of the Communist Party and for agrarian reform and other basic reforms. After a series of fiery speeches, the president signed two decrees. One expropriated oil refineries that were not yet controlled by Petrobras; the second declared that all underused property was now subject to expropriation and would be overseen by the new Superintendency of Agrarian Reform. It was announced that urban reform measures would soon follow and that the government would again send legislation to Congress to give the vote to illiterates and enlisted men.

The opposition responded with a massive antiregime rally and march in São Paulo. At the same time, in an unrelated move that contributed to the atmosphere of crisis, the increasingly aggressive Sailors' Association demanded better pay and respect for their political rights. The minister of the navy ordered the arrest of the association's directors. A protest meeting by the sailors was organized the following day at the headquarters of the metalworkers union. The minister cordoned off the hall and asked for backing from the First Army, bringing about a temporary settlement. But the minister then decided to resign as a matter of honor. His replacement decided not to punish the rebels. The military high command saw this as yet another act of insubordination and a direct challenge to the hierarchy.

Foolishly, the president decided to address a meeting of sergeants in Rio de Janeiro. This, too, was interpreted as presidential support for insubordination—something that the high command could not and would not tolerate. Troops mobilized on March 31 with the purpose of overthrowing the government. Goulart returned to Brasília on April 1, but in the face of overwhelming opposition he abandoned the capital and flew to Porto Alegre. The presidency was declared vacant, and the president of the Chamber of Deputies was sworn in as acting president. The general expectation was that after a short period, the armed forces would return power to the anti-Goulart civilian political elite. That expectation was wrong. The armed forces, drawing on years of discussion, planning, and debate, decided that it was time, once and for all, to modernize and deradicalize Brazil.

4

The 1964 Revolution:
From Bureaucratic Authoritarianism
to *Abertura*

I n the hours following João Goulart's flight from Brasília, there
was widespread uncertainty about what would happen next.
Some in Congress believed that the armed forces would hold power
briefly and then transfer executive authority to an acceptable civilian
political figure. Others thought that the military would hold new elections after banning some individuals from running for office. But the
speculation ended quickly. It soon became clear that the military and
its civilian supporters—including business leaders, the middle class, and
landowners—had decided that it was time for a regime change.

The coalition that overthrew President Goulart was convinced that
Brazil was confronting a number of crises in 1964. The country, they
believed, was heading for a leftist or communist takeover. The political
class was deeply divided and perceived as increasingly polarized and
unable to govern. The economy was in shambles as a result of incom-
petent and dangerous mismanagement. Consequently, they argued, the
old politics and failed economic policies required drastic surgery.

The solution was a bureaucratic-authoritarian government. Bureaucratic authoritarianism, a concept introduced by Argentine political scientist Guillermo O'Donnell, describes a form of dictatorship that is
associated primarily with an institution, notably the military, rather
than an individual. The primary goals of such regimes have typically
been economic growth and the preservation of order. In the Brazilian
case, bureaucratic authoritarianism took the form of an efficient public

55

sector, or "smart state," overseen by the armed forces. The government was run primarily by civilians save for the areas of security and national defense. However, most of the key players chosen for senior government positions were associated with the Superior War College and its many years of debate and analysis about the appropriate development model for Brazil.

Institutional Changes Following the 1964 Revolution

This outcome was driven by an important debate within the winning coalition over the future of democratic institutions. The military was generally divided into two camps on this issue, as on many others. The "Sorbonne" group favored a general commitment to restoring full democracy after implementation of the required reforms. General Humberto de Alencar Castelo Branco was viewed as the principal spokesman for this position. The so-called "hard-liners," led by General Artur Costa e Silva, favored a strong state with little, if any, civilian interference. The hard-liners believed that the military should retain political power for as long as necessary to repress the leftist threat and to restore law and order.

The Sorbonne contingent won the initial debate over the nature of the regime. It was decided to retain the 1946 constitution, but to modify it as needed to govern. Congress and other political institutions, including elections, would remain in place. Modifications would be made to ward off threats to the regime, but the commitment to formal democratic institutions would remain in place until 1985 and the return to civilian government. This approach distinguished the Brazilian government from later bureaucratic-authoritarian regimes in Latin America, which typically shut down all democratic institutions and banned most forms of political participation. The Brazilian decision reflected the ethos of a majority of the officer corps, who believed that their moderating power should be exercised to protect democratic civilian rule. In their view, it was the role of the armed forces to ensure that civilian political leaders took their responsibility seriously and acted to maintain public order and administer a well-run democratic state.

In this role the leaders of the armed forces issued what they termed an "institutional act" in early April 1964. Under this act, the regime's first president—General Castelo Branco—was given far-reaching powers. Only the president had the authority to propose public spending bills. If Congress failed to act within thirty days on a bill submitted by the president, the bill automatically became law. Members of Congress were stripped of their immunity from prosecution, and the president was given the authority to cancel mandates and to suspend the political rights of political leaders for a period of ten years.[1] In addition, the first institutional act established the soon-to-be-infamous police and military investigations to deal with groups and individuals suspected of subversion or crimes against the state. Over time, the investigations gained far more power than originally envisioned and engaged extensively in torture and repression.

Some limits on state power were maintained initially. The press remained basically independent in the early years of the new regime, and while many people were arrested, the right to habeas corpus was still viable. But prominent opponents of the regime were dealt with harshly, particularly in the northeast. The National Student Union was closed and driven underground. The University of Brasília, a relatively new institution that was widely suspected of housing antirevolutionary professors and students, was invaded, and suspected dissidents were expelled. Peasant league leaders were persecuted. Unions were purged. Local and regional politicians suspected of supporting the leftist movement before 1964 lost their rights, and many were jailed. Judges and members of Congress identified with the Goulart government were targeted and lost their positions. Within the armed forces, individuals who were viewed as untrustworthy because of past political sympathies or their active support for the Goulart government were forced out.

In June 1964 the government established the National Information Bureau (SNI) to coordinate these activities. Its mandate was to stifle internal subversion and to conduct counterintelligence. Over time, the SNI and its head, General Golbery do Couto e Silva, would become a parallel government subject to little formal oversight, and the willingness of one of Brazil's last military presidents to reduce the SNI's power would prove to be a critical turning point in the evolution of the bureaucratic-authoritarian regime.

New Economic Policies

After law and order, economic policy was the next priority for the new regime. As Werner Baer notes,

> The new military regime concluded that the path to economic recovery lay in control of inflation, elimination of accumulated price distortions, modernization of capital markets, creation of a system of incentives to

direct investments into sectors deemed essential by the government, attraction of foreign investments to expand the country's productive capacity, and expansion of public investments in infrastructure projects and heavy industry.[2]

To implement this approach, military leaders placed responsibility for economic recovery in the hands of technocrats associated with the Superior War College. Planning Minister Roberto Campos and Finance Minister Octávio Gouvêia de Bulhões were given the mandate to "fix" the economy and restore order to the country's public finances. The framework for their task was provided by the Government Economic Action Program (PAEG), which emphasized stabilization and market-oriented structural reforms. The ministers moved quickly to control the public deficit by reducing expenditures. States were prohibited from contracting debt without approval from Brasília, subsidies were slashed for basic products, and tax collection was increased. Salary adjustments were designed to keep wage growth below the rate of inflation, salaried urban workers were forced to surrender the right to lifelong employment they had previously earned after ten years of service, and Congress approved antistrike legislation that made legal work stoppages impossible. In addition, Campos and Bulhões made exports a top priority, reversing previous policy, and encouraged foreign direct investment by removing regulations that inhibited capital flows.

These policies imposed a high cost on the average worker, both in the cities and in the countryside, but they eventually paid off. The public deficit dropped sharply from 4.3 percent of GDP in 1963 to 0.3 percent in 1971. Inflation fell from close to 90 percent in 1964 to about 20 percent for the rest of the decade (see figure 4-1). Other governments and international institutions were quick to reward these achievements, and Brazil received financial support from the International Monetary Fund (IMF) and the U.S. government under President Lyndon B. Johnson. In macroeconomic terms, the Campos-Bulhões team passed the test with flying colors.

Breakthrough for the Hard-Liners

But while the PAEG and its administrators were hard at work fixing the economy, the political situation deteriorated rapidly. While the use of torture had been seemingly reduced since 1964, people still suddenly

FIGURE 4-1. **Percentage Change in GDP and the Consumer Price Index, 1960–84**

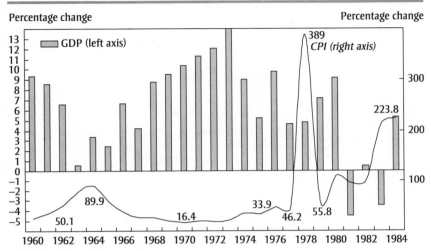

Source: Werner Baer, *The Brazilian Economy: Growth and Development*, 6th ed. (Boulder, Colo.: Lynne Rienner, 2008).

disappeared. And when coupled with concern about government repression, the tough economic measures pursued by Campos and Bulhões began to turn previously enthusiastic supporters into naysayers. The first test for the regime came in July 1965, when direct elections for state governors were held in eleven states. Even though the hard-liners had banned some suspected dissidents from running, the perceived opposition won in several key states, most significantly Minas Gerais and the former state of Guanabara.[3] This defeat for the government tipped the balance in favor of the hard-liners. The "go soft" approach of Castelo Branco and his backers at the Superior War College was rejected. The armed forces insisted on action.

The result was a second institutional act stipulating that the president and vice president would henceforth be elected indirectly by Congress. The president also gained additional national security authority, and the government was given the power to use decree-laws to bypass the legislature. Perhaps most dramatic was the decision to abolish the existing political party system, which hard-liners had long attacked as the root cause of Brazil's ungovernability. Legislation was approved to create two new parties: one representing the government and a second weaker organization collecting the "oppositions." The National Alliance for Renewal (ARENA) absorbed the National Democratic Union and the more conservative members of the old Social Democratic Party. The Brazilian Democratic Movement (MDB) represented the Labor Party and the more progressive Social Democratic Party.

The government also approved a new constitution in January 1967, having decided that the 1946 document failed to meet the needs of the revolution. Indirect elections for president and vice president were held in early 1967, and the hard-liners' candidate, war minister General Artur Costa e Silva, emerged as the winner. The Superior War College was pushed to the side, and a new version of the 1964 revolution took office in March 1967.

The regime's leaders believed that they had successfully overcome the opposition by adopting a new constitution, restructuring the party system, and installing a hard-line president. But they were quickly proved wrong. The year 1967 began a long and often bloody confrontation between opposition movements, both legal and subversive, and the bureaucratic-authoritarian regime. This cat-and-mouse game would last nearly twenty years.

The Second Phase of the 1964 Revolution: Protest and Violence

Initially, Costa e Silva sought to establish himself as a populist and "social humanist." He listened to dissent. He encouraged the formation of pro-government unions. While a staunch adherent of a strong state, he seemed to believe in limited liberalization. However, that commitment was soon tested, as resentment of the government grew despite a flourishing economy.

The Economic Miracle

The PAEG team had made significant progress against inflation, but growth rates were low and the social costs of the adjustment program remained very high. The Costa e Silva government, under the tutelage of a dynamic young economist from São Paulo, Antônio Delfim Netto, chose to alter course and encourage growth by prioritizing the role of the state in the economy through policies such as increased state expenditures, export incentives, investment in state enterprises, and the creation of government programs. Taken with many of the stabilization reforms of 1964,

Brazil saw "miracle" growth during the period between 1968 and 1973. After average annual growth rates of 3.7 percent under Campos, Delfim's program resulted in GDP annual growth rates that averaged 11.3 percent. The middle class flourished for the first time in decades. Overseas, the miracle gave Brazil an international luster that it had hoped for but never achieved; at home, it briefly dampened political opposition.

Industry was the leading sector after 1967, expanding at an average annual rate of 12.6 percent. Within the manufacturing sector, very high growth rates were achieved in transport equipment, machinery, and electric equipment, while the traditional sectors of textiles, clothing, and food products grew much more slowly. Initially, investment lagged behind manufacturing growth due to the existence of significant excess capacity and a low capital coefficient. But in the first half of the 1970s, as the miracle kicked in and this inherited slack disappeared, many businesses were challenged to make new investments for the first time in many years. In addition, Delfim's program provided for massive state investment in both infrastructure projects and heavy industry.

During this period agricultural production declined as a share of GDP, and the shares of industry and services grew about equally. Brazil's export profile diversified, and capital goods made up an increasing share of imports as the commitment to industrialization deepened. External trade grew at a higher rate than the economy as a whole. In the last years of the miracle, the average yearly growth rate of exports was 14.7 percent, while imports increased at an annual average rate of 21 percent. It is no surprise that Brazil's trade deficit grew rapidly. But Delfim's backers regarded this as a minor issue since it was easily covered by a dramatic increase in inflows of official and private capital.

By the early to mid-1970s, the miracle had drawn widespread international attention. Brazil's economic success was particularly striking when contrasted with the experience of its neighbors, where bureaucratic-authoritarian regimes were performing miserably. (The exception was Chile, where Salvador Allende was overthrown in September 1973 and replaced by the Pinochet government and the famous "Chicago Boys," who transformed the country's economy.)[4] That was the good news.

Growing Dissent within Civil Society

But there was also bad news. Beginning in 1967, despite the onset of the economic miracle, popular distaste for the regime increased dramatically. The middle class, which generally benefited from the miracle, remained quiescent, as it had for many years. But growing opposition came from two sources: segments of elite society and armed insurrectionaries.

The opposition began slowly but grew strongly with the widespread perception that the hard-liners and the SNI in particular were becoming increasingly repressive and acting with impunity. Leading the charge in opposing the military regime was the Roman Catholic Church. A leader in the antigovernment movement was Dom Hélder Câmara, who was appointed as the archbishop of Recife and Olinda shortly after the revolution. Hélder remained a thorn in the side of the revolution until it ended in 1985. Although he was banned from appearing in the Brazilian media, he became a charismatic spokesman for civil liberties and democracy in Brazil all over the world.

The student movement—the National Student Union—also regrouped, although it remained illegal, and became a very effective agent for mobilizing public protest against the government. Segments of the middle class began to turn against the government, as did representatives of the business sector. The new opposition party—the MDB—slowly but surely gained support. Workers began to strike and defy the government, beginning in 1968. Carlos Lacerda, who had been discarded by the regime after 1964, even tried to organize a "broad front" of senior political leaders—including Goulart, Kubitschek, and others—against the established order. The effort ultimately failed, but it indicated that important civilian leaders were willing to take on Brasília, even though it was a losing cause.

From the military point of view, the most serious challenge came from a sudden explosion of guerrilla activities. Several groups broke with the Communist Party of Brazil and turned to armed struggle in the late 1960s. Some of these movements included leftist military men. Bombs were planted in foreign consulates. Kidnappings and bank robberies became common. Finally, in reaction to a speech in Congress that was considered to be an insult to the armed services, the regime reacted. Congress was closed in December 1968. A new, very punitive institutional act was issued. The president received authority to act without regard to constitutional norms. The intelligence community assumed the leadership of the regime's effort to defeat the guerrilla groups by any means.

The most dramatic challenge to the government came in September 1969 with the kidnapping in Rio de Janeiro of the American ambassador. The government was forced to negotiate with the terrorists. In exchange for the life of the ambassador, several jailed guerrillas were released and allowed to leave Brazil to go into exile. Furious, the military determined to eradicate further armed insurrection.

The American ambassador's seizure took place a few days after President Costa e Silva suffered a stroke, launching a crisis of leadership. Judging him incapacitated and unable to return to duty, the high command proceeded to declare the presidency vacant and to appoint a military successor to Costa e Silva, ignoring the sitting civilian vice president. A poll of the senior commanders quickly identified General Emílio Garrastazu Médici as their top choice. Médici was respected across the military hierarchy. He was also a former director of the SNI, which proceeded under his presidency to eliminate the guerrillas with efficiency and brutality.

The Médici Years

General Médici took office as president in October 1969. A little more than a year later, new federal, state, and municipal elections took place. Frightened by the upsurge in urban guerrilla activity, middle-class voters decided that caution was the best strategy and voted overwhelmingly for ARENA. Faced with the Médici government's determination to permit no criticism, civil society retreated. Good economic times eased its flight.

Ironically, the Médici government was the most repressive of the governments that ruled Brazil after 1964, yet it was probably the most popular. Médici and his wife cut elegant figures at the race track and on social occasions. A new economic elite emerged from the country's economic miracle and indulged in conspicuous consumption. Urban modernization programs created a "new" Rio de Janeiro that satisfied domestic pride. The increasingly positive image of Brazil abroad, despite international press coverage of the regime's repression, bolstered Brazilian nationalism.

Médici and his fellow hard-liners basked in the success of the revolution and ignored its darker side. The benefits of the miracle were increasingly unevenly distributed. As Lincoln Gordon notes, the frequent assertion that " 'the poor got poorer' during these years . . . is not correct; they became less poor, while the rich became substantially richer."[5] But there were glaring errors and omissions in overall policy planning, which was guided by the 1971 First National Development Plan. Little if any attention was paid to rural development. The main effort in this area was the construction of a Trans-Amazon highway that was built to move poor folk from the backward northeast to the Amazon region. (Military hard-liners believed that Brazil needed to populate its vast hinterland to avoid a threat from its neighbors.) It failed in that goal, but the project did open the way to growing penetration of the Amazon valley, a process that had serious environmental implications and posed new threats to the region's indigenous peoples. Similarly, the government supported the building of a vast highway system that radiated north and west from Brasília. This network served primarily to draw poor farmers from the south of Brazil, who had been dispossessed by agro-industry, to move into the Amazon valley. The result was an increase in "slash and burn" agriculture that contributed to the further degradation of the valley. Finally, as part of the *Grandeza* strategy, huge hydroelectric plants, with international financing, were built in the center of the country, again damaging Brazil's natural environment.

The Transition Begins

Despite Médici's popularity, his hard-line backers were unable to control the succession process when attention turned to the selection of a new president in 1973. Within the armed forces, the increasingly imperious nature of the SNI and the excesses of the regime led many to favor a more moderate candidate. Their choice was General Ernesto Geisel, a former head of Petrobras and a confirmed supporter of the Superior War College. A newly created electoral college elected him as president, over an MDB candidate, in January 1974. Three months later he was sworn into office.

It became quickly apparent that the days of unending growth were over. The trigger was the Arab oil embargo in late 1973. Brazil imported 80 percent of its petroleum needs. The Organization of Petroleum Exporting Countries (OPEC), in retaliation for the military action taken against Arab states, suddenly and dramatically caused the price of petroleum to quadruple. The Geisel administration faced a difficult set of decisions. One strategy would sharply slow growth in order to reduce the country's bill for non-oil imports; the other would move full speed ahead in pursuit of continued high rates of growth. The government understood that the latter strategy would bring about a decline in the country's foreign exchange reserves and probably an increase in its foreign debt burden. Faced with these choices, it opted for growth.

There were two fundamental reasons for the decision, neither of which was completely unreasonable at the time. First, the legitimacy of the 1964 regime was founded to a large degree on its economic success. Slower growth would quickly undermine the fragile but critical popular support the government enjoyed. Second, Geisel and SNI head Golbery had concluded that the time had come for an opening of the political system, or *abertura*. It was a precarious plan given the continued strength of the hard-liners, but it would undoubtedly be easier if the economy remained a strong card in the hands of the presidential palace.

The Second National Development Plan

Geisel's economic team decided that a new push to deepen growth was needed. The Second National Development Plan (PND II, 1975–79) took several decisions that appeared audacious in the face of rising oil prices and the inevitability of an increase in the level of government indebtedness.[6] The state-driven investment plan emphasized the import substitution of basic industrial products such as steel, copper, fertilizers, and petrochemicals. It also sought to expand the physical infrastructure of the country by investing in hydroelectric and nuclear power plants, transportation and communication grids, and alcohol production (as a potential substitute for gasoline). The government hoped that these decisions would draw foreign direct investment and support from multilateral banks, such as the World Bank, allow sustained economic growth, allow Brazil to avoid defaulting on its external debt, and prepare the country for a deeper and more diversified commitment to export-led industrialization.

The overall strategy worked reasonably well in that economic growth rates remained in the 7 percent range for the remainder of the decade. But to finance PND II, Brazil needed to borrow abroad. The country's debt burden grew very quickly. The argument in Brasília was simple: Growth via debt was feasible because PND II would ultimately produce large trade surpluses that would permit the government to service its international debt obligations. This, again, was not totally unreasonable in 1974–75. Real world interest rates were negative and remained so until 1978 (see table 4-1); commercial banks were keen to recycle the petrodollars that OPEC countries were depositing in international commercial banks; and as a result there was an ample supply of cash, which Brazil's government and state-owned companies were happy to absorb.

Abertura: *The Political Tides Gradually Change*

With their economic choices made, Geisel and Golbery turned their attention to the delicate issue of political liberalization and redemocratization. Both Geisel and Golbery believed that military rule was transitional and that a gradual shift toward civilian rule should take place.

TABLE 4-1. **Real International Interest Rates, 1974–84**

Percent

Year	U.S. nominal prime rate	U.S. real prime rate
1974	10.81	−2.2
1975	7.86	−2.9
1976	6.84	−1.3
1977	6.83	−1.4
1978	9.06	1.7
1979	12.67	3.2
1980	15.27	3.0
1981	18.85	8.1
1982	14.77	6.8
1983	10.81	5.5
1984	12.04	6.9

Source: Patrice Franko, *The Puzzle of Latin American Development* (Lanham, Md.: Rowman and Littlefield, 2007), table 4.2, p. 82, based on data from United Nations Economic Commission for Latin America and the Caribbean, *Economic Survey of Latin America and the Caribbean* (Santiago: ECLAC, various years) and International Monetary Fund, *International Financial Statistics, 1987* (Washington: IMF, 1987).

Most important, during this period censorship of the press was lifted, and the fifth institutional act was abolished.[7] Why? The president and his chief adviser were sensitive to the growing vigor of the civilian opposition and to growing concern about torture in Brazil, which had been receiving increased attention in the world press. There was also growing pressure for liberalization from within the Brazilian population.[8] But the main driver of change was changing sentiment within the armed forces. After being ousted by the hard-liners in 1967, the Sorbonne group was back in the presidential palace. Geisel and Golbery understood that a significant portion of the military leadership was tiring of being seen as torturers. Many military leaders were dismayed by the growth in influence of the SNI, whose leadership, while drawn from the traditional military command pool, often acted as a separate military and political force. As this revulsion deepened, support for a decision to "return the military to the barracks" gained ground.

Political scientist Alfred Stepan distinguishes between the military as an institution and the military as government. The government role had not traditionally been part of the portfolio of the Brazilian armed forces. While it had exercised a moderating role several times after the fall of the Brazilian empire in 1889, the military had never assumed the role of government until 1964.[9] The decision to retain political power with the collapse of the Goulart government heightened tensions within the institution. President Castelo Branco had wanted to preside over a "tutelary democracy," which would prepare the way for an eventual return to "rational and true democracy" at some point in the future.[10] Other elements in the armed forces disdained formal democracy and favored a more authoritarian approach to governance without any necessary timetable for the restoration of civilian, democratic rule.

This debate continued into the 1970s. The decision of Geisel and Golbery to implement a strategy of withdrawal was not popular with many in the military, but the tensions between the SNI and the traditional forces, the slowdown in the economy associated with the oil crisis, and the rise of a legitimate civilian opposition movement carried the day in favor of ending the experiment with military government.

The growing strength of the opposition became evident in November 1974, when the MDB made significant gains in elections for Congress, particularly in the large cities and the more developed states in the southeast. It gained further force in October 1975, when Vladimir Herzog, a well-known editor for the state television channel in São Paulo, was taken into custody by the counterintelligence forces and died. The incident was a turning point for public attitudes toward repression, the Catholic Church issued a stinging criticism of the regime, and for the first time the National Bar Association called for a return to a state of law. In January 1976 a metalworker died in similar circumstances to Herzog. In a bold and unexpected move, Geisel fired the hard-line commanding general in São Paulo and replaced him with an individual committed to liberalization. This move signaled to the officer corps that the president was in charge of the government and expected the military to respect his decisions.

The remaining years of the Geisel government were dedicated to the slow and careful process of *abertura*. Municipal elections in November 1976 again showed large gains for the MDB. In response, to head off a rebellion by hard-liners, Geisel recessed Congress in April 1977 and took steps to create a set of reforms, known as the "April Package,"[11] that would keep ARENA in the majority. But at the same time, the president signaled to reformers that his commitment to political opening remained in place by calling for dialogue with the opposition and the Catholic Church. And when the MDB emerged as the big winner in legislative elections in 1978, the government accepted the results of the balloting.

In addition, Geisel and Golbery accepted limited worker mobilization, even in the countryside. When the Catholic Church created a Pastoral Land Commission that took an active role in the countryside, encouraging political and civic organizations, the presidential palace looked the other way, as long as there was no subversive threat that the hard-liners could use to justify a crackdown. The government also tolerated the emergence of a "new unionism" in and around São Paulo. With the dramatic increase in industrialization in the 1970s, a new and younger workforce appeared on the factory floor and soon contested the state-run organization of labor. The new union movement, which received strong support from the Catholic Church and other civil society groups, successfully organized a series of slowdowns and strikes in 1978 and 1979. The striking workers not only wanted their wages restored but also demanded recognition for factory committees and, more broadly, democratic freedoms. They were led by the metalworkers union, headed by Luiz Inácio da Silva, known as Lula.

Near the end of Geisel's term in 1978, he and Golbery could reflect with some pride on their accomplishments. The hard-liners had been contained, if not eliminated. Personal freedoms had been restored. Under Geisel, censorship was reduced and the military's use of torture was restrained. The institutional act of 1964, which allowed for far-reaching military engagement in political and civilian affairs, was abolished, and habeas corpus and political liberties were restored. In addition, Congress experienced increased autonomy from the executive branch.[12] The liberalization process was well under way, but it was not complete. That, they hoped, would be the main task of the next government.

The Debt Crisis

The selection of a new chief executive took place amid growing social and political mobilization. Nonetheless, Geisel and Golbery were able to mastermind the selection of General João Batista Figueiredo, a former head of the SNI who was acceptable to both the Superior War College and to most, if not all, the hard-liners. Figueiredo was duly elected president by the electoral college in October 1978, only to confront a perilous economic and political situation.

Lured by extraordinarily attractive international prices for capital, Brazil had accumulated considerable external debt over the years (see figure 4-2.) By 1979 its debt service burden was equal to more than 63 percent of the country's exports. The task of tackling this burden fell to

FIGURE 4-2. Current Account and Gross Debt, 1960–84

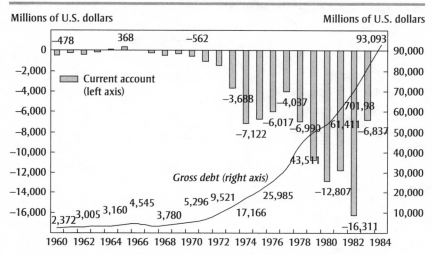

Source: Werner Baer, *The Brazilian Economy: Growth and Development*, 6th ed. (Boulder, Colo.: Lynne Rienner, 2008), p. 408.

Mário Henrique Simonsen, a highly respected economist and finance minister under Geisel, who was appointed planning minister with overall responsibility for economic strategy in early 1979. Simonsen favored an immediate slowdown in growth to address both the balance-of-payments deficit and inflation. He called for liberalization of imports, stricter control of spending by state-owned companies, and a reduction of general credit subsidies. It was a reasonable economic agenda, except that it was opposed by most of his colleagues in the government, who were committed to spending and not saving. The business community feared a contraction. There were worries over labor unrest since wages were being eroded by inflation. In despair, Simonsen resigned in August 1979, to be replaced by the author of the miracle, Antônio Delfim Netto. The appointment was met with euphoria by the private sector, which expected the miracle years to return.

But circumstances had changed dramatically, both globally and internally, since the decade of *Grandeza*. The global economic recession that began with the second oil crisis, in the wake of the 1979 Iranian revolution, had severe implications for Brazil, as for most developing countries. World demand fell, commodity prices declined, commercial banks in the United States, Europe, and Japan became reluctant to lend, and world

FIGURE 4-3. Current Account Balance, External Debt, and International Reserves, 1980–85

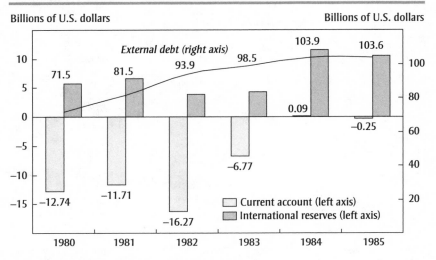

Source: Economist Intelligence Unit, "Brazil Country Finance" (London: EIU, 2009).

interest rates shot up, making borrowing expensive and debt repayment suddenly much more challenging. Brazil's short-term obligations rose sharply, while its foreign exchange reserves declined (see figure 4-3). The Figueiredo administration entered a period of constant improvisation and crisis management that would last until it left office in 1985.

Delfim was forced to adopt an austerity program in December 1979. It consisted of a currency devaluation, the elimination of export subsidies, an increase in the price of public services, temporary taxes on windfall gains in agricultural exports, the abolition of the Law of Similars, and the elimination of deposit requirements on capital flows.[13] Inflation and wage demands increased. The external deficit became ever more difficult to finance. The government implemented a second austerity program in late 1980. As a result, GDP and investment declined.

A further blow fell when Mexico declared a moratorium on its debt payments in August 1982. International financial markets, which were critical to financing the overall debt burden of the region, contracted. The Brazilian government faced a dramatic liquidity crisis by the end of the year. The government was forced to approach the IMF for help in December 1982, after refusing to do so for many years. Successive governments had refused to accept the notorious conditionality linked to IMF lending. The conditions were deemed to be too onerous and a violation of Brazil's sovereignty. This time, the government had no choice. In return for its financial support, the IMF called on Brazil to raise the real exchange rate; reduce domestic demand by finding ways to reduce private consumption, investment, and public expenditures; and increase the collection of taxes. The government was also forced to eliminate subsidies for exports. The removal of the subsidies required a stepped-up devaluation of the currency as a compensating measure, further increasing the burden on firms with foreign debt.

This austerity program remained in effect throughout 1984. By then, after initially contracting, the Brazilian economy began to rebound. GDP growth in 1984 was almost 6 percent, the trade balance was more than $11 billion in the black (after being negative from 1980 through 1982), and the country's reserves were recovering. However, inflation had reached 200 percent, external debt reached an all-time high of $104 billion (or 52 percent of GDP), and the public sector deficit was climbing. From 3 percent of GDP in 1982, it grew to a peak of 17.5 percent of GDP in 1989.

Return to Civilian Government

Meanwhile, despite the unpropitious economic climate, the Figueiredo government sought to move ahead with political liberalization. In August 1979 it issued an amnesty law that was approved by Congress. The legislation reached out to the opposing camps by both giving protection to the hard-liners who had been responsible for torture and allowing many political exiles to return to Brazil. Four months later, in an effort to defuse the seemingly unstoppable electoral gains of the MDB, the government decided to abolish both ARENA and the MDB. The result was a new political party system in 1980. ARENA became the Democratic Social Party (PDS), but its days of glory were gone forever. The MDB added "party" to its name and emerged as the PMDB, the great catch-all party of succeeding decades. The third major new party was the Workers Party (PT), which represented rural and urban workers as well as a coalition of opposition forces including the Catholic Church, students, and the professional middle class. The Workers Party was particularly strong in the São Paulo industrial belt; one of its most prominent leaders was Lula, the head of the metalworkers union. Ironically, the union movement split as the Workers Party was being formed. One group chose to work closely with the PT; the other, more moderate in temperament and tone, created a rival organization.

Legislative elections were held as scheduled in November 1982. While the PDS won majorities in both chambers of Congress, the opposition won in the important states of São Paulo, Minas Gerais, and Rio de Janeiro. The PT, which fared poorly in the polling, began to rally its supporters behind the idea of a return to direct presidential elections, as the PMDB decided to pursue the same strategy. Because direct elections favored the number of voters within a state rather than its population, states with smaller but more literate populations performed favorably, which benefited the PT because its supporters were located mostly in cities and suburbs.[14] The opposition movements organized a series of nationwide rallies that drew tens of thousands of enthusiastic supporters to voice their support for "Direct Elections Now" or *"Direitas Ja."* However, a constitutional amendment authorizing direct election of the president required a two-thirds majority in Congress for passage. While approved by a majority, it failed to clear this hurdle.

Following their loss, the opposition movements sought an alternative strategy. The decision was taken to confront the military regime on its own turf, the electoral college, when it came time to choose a new president in 1985. As the balloting approached, the ruling PDS chose former mayor, governor, and deputy Paulo Maluf as the status quo candidate. The traditional opposition, in the form of the PMDB, joined forces with the new Liberal Front Party, which was led by Vice President Aureliano Chaves, to campaign jointly under the banner of the Democratic Alliance. This new grouping chose Tancredo Neves, a seasoned and respected politician from Minas Gerais, as its presidential standard bearer. To the discomfort of many, it also chose José Sarney, who had recently served as president of the PDS, as its candidate for vice president.

The electoral college met in Brasília on January 15, 1985, and the opposition ticket easily defeated the PDS. The president-elect immediately began to plan the transition to power on March 15. After a traditional trip abroad, Tancredo prepared for the inauguration but was taken ill the night before. Vice President Sarney was sworn in as temporary chief executive. It was assumed Tancredo would recover quickly and return to Brasília, but after a series of controversial medical procedures, he died in São Paulo in April. Brazil was suddenly confronted with a new president with little political support within the new government. A transition very different from what Brazilians had expected and anticipated was about to begin.

5
The Incomplete Transition, 1985–94

In politics, timing is often critical. Brazil was unlucky in the timing of its return to civilian government in March 1985. Tancredo Neves, the president elect, was viewed as a potential miracle worker. He had been active in state and national politics for decades and was seen as a wise elder statesman just right for the job at hand. His sudden death in April shocked the country. The ill-prepared and not particularly popular vice president, José Sarney, inherited a complicated and increasingly precarious situation. Sarney had been a stalwart of the military regime. Tancredo had asked him to serve as his running mate to persuade more conservative, pro-regime supporters to vote for the opposition ticket. The strategy worked. But no one ever thought that Sarney would become chief executive.

The incoming Sarney administration found itself buffeted from all sides by pressure for immediate structural changes in both the political and economic spheres. The newly empowered civilian political class wanted to roll back much of the centralized decisionmaking of the military regime. They also wanted to introduce a reform agenda that would appeal to the public. However, the political realities complicated the situation.

Sarney now presided over a heterogeneous coalition dominated by the Brazilian Democratic Movement Party (PMDB), the old opposition party during the military years. Its junior partner, the Party of the Liberal Front (PFL), was more conservative and based primarily in the northeast, one of Brazil's poorest regions. The first contentious issue that confronted the new government was what to do with the authoritarian constitution of 1969, which was still the law of the land. Part of the ruling coalition wanted to elect a constituent assembly to write a new document as quickly as possible. A second group favored postponing the constitutional revision process, perhaps electing the assembly during the congressional and gubernatorial elections scheduled for November 1986. The former option was supported by those who wanted to abandon the authoritarian legacy immediately; the latter believed the new government needed time to consolidate its position, particularly after the loss of Tancredo Neves. Sarney opted for the later date and decided that the Congress elected in November 1986 would also serve as the assembly. To satisfy the political faction that wanted an election to be held sooner, the president appointed a "commission of notables" to draft a new constitution that would serve as a point of departure in early 1987.

To indicate that his government would act democratically, Sarney decided that he would not use many of the authoritarian devices in the existing constitution, such as the prerogative of the president to send a bill to Congress with a time limit within which the Congress had to act or the bill would be passed automatically. Given the diversity of parties and personalities in the Congress, it was almost impossible to consider and vote on a measure within the specified time limit (thirty or forty-five days). The president also promised not to use the power of presidential decree, which the military regime had used frequently to bypass the legislature. These were goodwill gestures; until a new constitution was written and approved, those powers remained at the disposal of the president, to be used at his discretion.

Another thorny issue was the cabinet that had been selected carefully by Tancredo Neves. Given his relative weakness politically, Sarney decided to maintain the Neves cabinet. The ministers reflected the relative strength of the major parties in the Congress—a nine to four majority for the PMDB. Five of the new ministers had seen the military strip them of their elective office or their political rights or both. It was unclear whether they were in a position to "forgive and forget" or whether they would use their new powers to seek revenge. Ultimately, cooler heads prevailed, and the group chose to put the military regime's decisions in the past. The cabinet also held contradictory policy views. The minister of agriculture favored a radical land reform program, but it was clear that the conservative political forces in the country, which included the military high command, would reject such an initiative. The campaign had promised to address the country's difficult social agenda, but the finance minister, a nephew of Neves, was a fiscal conservative and publicly supported an orthodox approach to reviving the economy.

To demonstrate his independence, Francisco Neves Dornelles, the finance minister, announced a 10 percent cut in public spending, a two-month suspension of all government bank lending, and a one-year freeze on all public sector hiring. A majority of the Congress was considerably unhappy with these policies. After twenty-one years of dictatorship, they wanted to demonstrate to their constituents, prior to the November 1986 elections, that they were responsive to built-up expectations. That translated into a great deal of money for social spending at the local level. The planning minister was also concerned that Dornelles's policies might cause an economic slowdown or even a recession.

These differences could have paralyzed the new government, but Sarney was smart enough to negotiate a political pact with Ulysses Guimarães, the head of the PMDB, to seek compromise in order to consolidate the democratic transition. Electoral politics were the order of the day, and attention was focused on the elections scheduled for the following year. With the agreement as background, Sarney announced that the government would meet its foreign debt commitments, but not at the cost of social deprivation at home. While fiscal and monetary austerity would remain in place, there would be an immediate emergency program to aid the poorest segments of society.

In early May the Congress approved, and the president signed, a series of measures aimed at reviving democratic political institutions. Direct presidential elections were restored, eliminating the electoral college through which the military had controlled the presidential succession until 1985. Illiterates were given the right to vote. All political parties that met the minimal registration requirements were legalized. The principal beneficiaries were Brazil's two communist parties—the orthodox, Moscow-oriented organization and a dissident entity, more radical and smaller than the principal communist organization. To open the political process further, free and direct elections of mayors were allowed for all cities; the election was set for November 15, 1985.

The political landscape was complicated by the wide array of political parties that had resulted from the creation of a multiparty system in 1979. While the PMDB, the original party of opposition to the military dictatorship, was viewed as the major party, it was followed by an array of organizations of ill-defined ideology that were strongly personalist and often regional in nature. In the November 1985 mayoral elections, the PMDB won 19 of the 25 capitals and 110 of the 201 other cities, but lost four key elections. In São Paulo, the industrial heartland, former president Jânio Quadros, who had resigned suddenly in August 1961, defeated future president Fernando Henrique Cardoso; in Rio de Janeiro a candidate supported by Leonel Brizola, the brother-in-law of former president João Goulart and a key opponent of the military regime, was elected easily; non-PMDB candidates also won in the important cities of Porto Alegre and Recife.

Analysts commented that personalities, such as Quadros and Brizola, were back in strength in the evolving political landscape. Populism was apparently alive and well with the reappearance of these two leaders. One trend was fairly clear—Brazilians had voted for the center-left. The old government party, the PSD (Social Democratic Party), was the big loser. But many observers raised an important question: Where was a new generation of politicians? The pre-1964 leaders were alive and well, but new faces were few and far between. Many thought that this was a perverse legacy of the years of military rule. Traditional politicians of the pre-1964 generation were able to work out an accommodation with the 1964 regime; younger men and women opted for other avenues of participation in civil society or at the municipal and state levels. This would become an important issue over the next decade or so, as the older generation dominated the national political landscape, often with ideas based in the past rather than in the future.

Foreign Debt and Inflation

One of the principal policy issues inherited by the Sarney administration was that of the country's foreign debt. Standing at $95 billion, it was the largest in the world. The policy question was whether Brazil could—or should—service the debt (inherited from the military) if doing so would endanger growth or preclude addressing pending social demands. Sarney entered office in the midst of the so-called "lost decade" of debt. With Mexico's default on its outstanding debt in the summer of 1982, private bank lending and bilateral aid basically stopped. In order to seek assistance from the International Monetary Fund (IMF), a government was expected—or forced—to accept often onerous conditions that were usually politically unpopular. Brazil began to negotiate with the IMF at the end of the Figueiredo government but was never able to come to a mutually satisfactory set of conditions to facilitate the release of funds.

Finance Minister Dornelles faced a dilemma. The economy had begun to improve in 1984; the balance of payments was positive, and the trade balance had reached a new high of $13.1 billion.[1] The increase was a result of the growth in exports and a drop in imports. It was estimated that the current trade surplus was equivalent to the outstanding interest on Brazil's foreign debt. The foreign trade position was supported by a strong foreign exchange reserve position. With these numbers in hand, Brazil was in a relatively good position to negotiate with its creditors. Forecasts for 1985 looked reasonably positive as well. For the moment, Brazil did not need the help of the IMF, postponing a negative political reaction if it had to deal with Washington. Instead, it chose to open discussions with the commercial banks that held about $35 billion of Brazilian loans that would fall due between 1985 and 1989. With careful negotiations, an agreement was reached in July 1985 that rolled over the principal due in 1985 and 1986 and renewed important trade credits.

New Ideas to Control Inflation: The Cruzado Plan

Along with the foreign debt issue, inflation remained a critical challenge. Werner Baer aptly characterizes this period as one of "inflation and economic drift."[2] As Lincoln Gordon observes, "The inflation rate per year averaged 34 percent in the 1970s, 428 percent in the 1980s, and almost 1,400 percent in the five years 1990–1994."[3] For average Brazilians, this meant an increasingly unacceptable standard of living, since their real wages eroded dramatically.

Extensive debate in academic and policy circles identified many culprits when it came to inflation, but few cures. The two oil shocks of the 1970s were clearly part of the problem, since the affected sectors were anxious to pass on their higher production costs. A dramatic increase in world interest rates in the early 1980s, from 6.8 percent in 1977 to 18.8 percent in 1981, was a contributing factor, as were the two maxi-devaluations of 1979 and 1983, which raised the burden of debt and the cost of imports. Brazil also experienced a series of natural disasters, including droughts and floods, that reduced the supply and raised the prices of a variety of crucial products, such as foodstuffs. Finally, in 1979 the government adopted a new wage law that was designed to increase the purchasing power of lower-wage groups, at the cost of yet more inflation.[4]

Lacking the political will to control spending, all branches of the government exceeded their budgets. As needed, the government printed money to meet its immediate obligations. Little, if any, consideration was given to fiscal responsibility as the political class sought to impress constituents with its ability to respond to pent-up demands for jobs, social support programs, and subsidized housing and health care. Some saw the appointment of a conservative finance minister, Francisco Dornelles, as a signal that fiscal austerity would be part of the new civilian government's program. But Dornelles stepped down in August 1985, taking with him any hope of an orthodox adjustment through fiscal and monetary austerity and close cooperation with the IMF.

Dornelles's replacement, São Paulo businessman Dilson Funaro, favored growth over austerity and was known to be critical of IMF demands for adjustment. He hoped to find an easy solution to the long-standing challenge of controlling inflation. Funaro had served as president of the National Bank of Economic and Social Development during the first months of the Sarney government. He was an industrialist from São Paulo who had been very active in the São Paulo Federation of Industries, a key opponent of the military regime. Funaro styled himself as a growth-oriented Keynesian, closer to the position of the planning minister, João Sayad, who had disagreed with Dornelles over economic policy from the beginning of the transition. He also was the first high-level São Paulo business leader to join the government in a senior position since 1964. His politics were correct, and his background suggested that he would provide strong leadership in the Ministry of Finance. He brought with him a group of young economists from the country's leading universities and charged them with finding a permanent solution to the inflation that had plagued Brazil for decades.

The media, think tanks, and other actors in civil society were demanding that the new government not repeat the mistakes of the military regime—inflation had to be tamed. As the prices of food and consumer durable goods increased almost daily, the political pressure on Brasília to act intensified. A school of thought that grew increasingly influential in government circles called for the end of indexation and argued that in an indexed economy like that of Brazil, past inflation became built in as "inertial inflation." The latter never declined, becoming the base on which new inflation was added. Deindexing the economy was the only logical step. The key question was how and when was the best political moment to do so.

The government was perplexed. The 1985 growth rate was an impressive 8.3 percent, but the inflation rate was 222 percent. Having avoided the IMF conditionality, which would have required a painful orthodox adjustment program, it decided to implement a heterodox (unorthodox) shock.[5] Driven in part by the falling popularity of the government, and its apparent inability to address the inflation issue, Funaro, President Sarney, and his economic team opted for a radical and largely untested experiment. A similar program had been tried in inflation-prone Argentina in 1985 and failed, but the Brazilians thought that their version would succeed with better planning and implementation.

The president, with much fanfare, announced the Cruzado Plan on national television on February 28, 1986:

> The President described inflation as 'public enemy number one' and called on all Brazilians to join in a 'war of life and death' against it. He invited his fellow citizens to make themselves price inspectors at their local stores, confronting any shopkeepers who raised their prices in violation of the price freeze.[6]

The basic elements of the program were initially attractive, including a radical monetary reform. It replaced the cruzeiro (at 1,000 to 1) with a new currency, the cruzado; indexation was abolished. There was a one-year freeze on mortgage rates and rents and an indefinite freeze on prices. There was also a wage freeze following a readjustment that set new real wages at an average of the previous six months plus 8 percent and set the minimum wage at 15 percent. Thereafter, a sliding scale would automatically adjust wages whenever inflation reached 20 percent from the previous adjustment or from annual base dates for specific categories. Workers were free to bargain with employers over further wage increases. Finally, an unemployment benefit was established wherein recipients would have to have a minimum employment record and contribute to the social security system. The program's target was the formal labor market, concentrated in the developed south and southeast of the country, where most people voted independently, in contrast to the north and northeast, where people were "voted" by local political bosses. The plan was an immediate winner with the public across the country. Inflation was tamed, and prices were stable for the first time in decades. Speculators were the losers; the average consumer was the winner (see box 5-1).[7]

> **B O X 5 - 1 . Cornerstones of the Cruzado Plan**
>
> —A general freeze on the price of final goods
> —A wage freeze following a readjustment that set the new real wages at the previous six months' average plus 8 percent and set the minimum wage at 15 percent
> —Application of the same formula to rents and mortgage payments, without the 8 percent increase
> —A wage-escalation system, which guaranteed an automatic wage increase each time the consumer price index rose 20 percent from the previous adjustment or from each category's annual "base date"
> —Prohibition of indexation clauses for contracts of less than one year
> —Creation of a new currency, the cruzado, which replaced the old cruzeiro (Cz$1 being equal to Cr$1,000). There was no specific reference in the decree-laws to the exchange rate, but the government clearly indicated that it intended to keep it fixed indefinitely at Cz$13.84 to the U.S. dollar.
>
> *Source:* Werner Baer, *The Brazilian Economy: Growth and Development*, 6th ed. (Boulder, Colo.: Lynne Rienner, 2008), p. 111.

Unfortunately, the plan was born with the seeds of its destruction embedded within it. Its authors knew that the price freeze had to be short-lived so that prices could once again help to allocate resources. But since the price freeze was the source of the Sarney government's new-found popularity, political criteria quickly trumped economic thinking. In the summer of 1986, economists and analysts called for price realignments, which the government ignored. The government overrode their advice in the hope of preserving its public support until November 1986, when national elections would take place. The success of the Cruzado Plan was expected to guarantee a massive victory for the ruling PMDB. Consumers went on a buying spree since prices were frozen. Real wage increases with no inflation were a novelty, especially for citizens in the center-south of the country. Indicators of excess demand appeared within weeks. Consumer durables sold immediately. Foreign travel increased dramatically. Soon shortages began to appear, especially of items such as meat. The expectations of the economic team were off target. Rather than accepting the new economic order calmly, Brazilians had a deep-seated fear of a return to inflation if price controls were lifted. Therefore, buy now and buy as much as possible appeared to be the choice of the day.

By July 1986, with November elections looming, Sarney took measures to reduce consumption and increase investment. The government decided to tax cars and foreign travel, items very popular with the middle class. Sales of new and used cars and of gasoline and alcohol would now be subject to a 20–25 percent compulsory tax refundable in three years. International air tickets were to carry a compulsory 25 percent tax, also refundable after three years. Any purchase of U.S. dollars would have a nonrefundable surcharge of 25 percent.

As these measures were being taken, the government economists were debating when to lift the price freeze. There was no consensus. Most were concerned that a premature unfreezing would reintroduce inflationary expectations and bring about renewed inertial conditions. But as the elections of November 1986 approached, political considerations replaced economic rationality. Zero inflation was the magic bullet that would give the PMDB a big majority in the forthcoming elections for Congress and the constituent assembly. But net direct foreign investment was disappointing; investors were increasingly skeptical regarding the "heterodoxy" of the shock program. Profit remittances and capital flight were rising—all wanted to get their money out of Brazil before a possible crash. An important reason, from the government's viewpoint, for retaining the price freeze was to avoid the "trigger" that allowed wages to rise automatically every time the accumulated inflation reached 20 percent.

With a rush to the finish line, the November elections gave the PMDB a massive electoral victory. But reality quickly set in, and Cruzado II was announced shortly after the election results were published. Prices were realigned for "middle-class" consumer goods, and taxes on them were increased. A crawling-peg exchange rate devaluation was reinstituted, and new tax incentives for savers were introduced. The goal was to dampen consumption expenditures. But as critics pointed out, the price increases tended to divert consumption expenditures rather than to stimulate savings. Inflation revived. Wages rose as the automatic trigger began to function. Inflationary expectations—and middle-class fear—reemerged. The international reserve position fell so low that the central bank declared a unilateral moratorium on existing debt obligations in February 1987. The euphoria of February 1986 gave way to anger and cynicism in February 1987 on the part of the average Brazilian.

The Bresser Plan

Under heavy criticism in both the public and the private sector, Funaro left office in April 1987 and was replaced by Luiz Carlos Bresser-Pereira, an economist who served earlier as president of the State Bank of São Paulo. He introduced the Bresser Plan, which adopted new price and wage freezes, this time with caps to be readjusted every three months. The plan also canceled the trigger mechanism for automatic wage increases, which had been an important element in the Cruzado Plan, and targeted interest rates above inflation to limit the overheating of the economy, a lesson learned from the experience of the Cruzado Plan. The exchange rate was kept in check through a series of mini-devaluations.

But the Bresser Plan failed in large part due to an absence of fiscal discipline. Bresser resigned in December 1987, and in January 1988 the Bresser Plan gave way to the "Rice and Beans" policy, a modest day-to-day effort by the new minister, Mailson da Nóbrega, to control prices and public spending. But by mid-1988 the economy was again in crisis, with inflation running at 81 percent a month by March 1990, investment slowing, GDP growing at barely over 1 percent, and unemployment on the rise. The government had no stomach for fiscal discipline, and the budget deficit exceeded 16 percent of annual output. The new constitution, which was promulgated in October 1988, made things worse by requiring the central government to transfer 21.5 percent of its income tax and manufactured goods tax revenue to state and municipal authorities by 1993. This measure helped members of Congress to strengthen their local political base. It also reflected a rejection of the centralizing measures taken during the military years. But the decrease in the federal government's resources was not matched by a reduction in its obligations, putting even more strain on the budget. Local and state governments became "fat" with funds, but little programmatic responsibility; the federal government became very "lean," while continuing to bear a heavy burden of earmarked and other program obligations.

Desperate for a turnaround, the government introduced yet another currency, the *cruzado novo*, as part of the January 1989 Summer Plan, but to little avail. The new plan was a shabby copy of its predecessors. There was a new price and wage freeze. Indexation was abolished, except for savings deposit accounts. An attempt was made to restrain monetary and credit expansion and devaluation of the exchange rate. The Summer Plan collapsed more quickly than the Rice and Beans Plan. The credibility of the government had disappeared. The public was exhausted from trying to understand the different and often contradictory policies of the government. The economy remained in disarray, and the Sarney government (which had its mandate extended to five years under the new constitution) limped to a close at the end of 1989. In his final months in office, the president rarely left the relative safety of Brasília and relied heavily on the symbolic support of the armed forces. When the first direct presidential election in almost thirty years was held on October 15, 1989, the electorate turned strongly against the ruling PMDB. Once viewed as the driving force behind the transition from military rule to democratic government, the PMDB was now fatally associated with the mismanagement and failure of the Sarney administration. As the major party in Congress, it was held responsible for the soaring inflation and dramatic fall in living standards that had hurt so much of the public.

Fernando Collor de Mello: Hope and Disillusion

In the run-up to the election, Fernando Collor de Mello, a little-known politician from a small northeastern state, captured the public's imagination. Tall, young, and photogenic, he seemed to offer a new departure in national politics. Collor campaigned against corruption and big government and for the modernization of the national economy. His main opponent was Luiz Inácio da Silva (known as Lula), the leader of the Workers Party (PT) and symbol of the new, independent unionism that had gained force in the 1970s (this would be the first of Lula's four attempts to be elected president; he would succeed on the fourth try in 2002).

Lula and the PT were viewed as a direct threat to the status quo. Their election platform frightened many voters with its call for radical reforms, including a moratorium on foreign debt payments, radical land reform, and a neo-Marxist, antimarket economic program. In contrast, although Collor was brash and disrespectful of many in the political establishment, he came from a family that belonged to the traditional power structure and was well known in regional politics. Collor's father had been a national senator for many years, and the family fortune had been made by working with the established economic and political forces in power in Brazil for many decades. Given a choice between a new face like Collor and a radical challenger to the status quo, the establishment

B O X   5 - 2 . Cornerstones of the Collor Plan

—Adoption of the fourth currency in four years, renaming it the cruzeiro, to replace the cruzado novo, with a conversion rate of 1:1
    —An eighteen-month freeze on a large part of savings and financial assets
    —A thirty-day wage and price freeze, with subsequent adjustments
    —A new wealth tax
    —The compulsory purchase by financial institutions of nonnegotiable "privatization certificates."

Source: Riordan Roett, *Brazil: Politics in a Patrimonial Society,* 5th ed. (Westport, Conn.: Praeger, 1999), p. 162.

reluctantly decided that Collor was the lesser of two evils. With the support of the main media outlets, including the powerful and conservative Globo television empire, he won in the second round of balloting with 53 percent of the vote.

However, Collor was handicapped by his lack of legislative support. His fledgling party, the National Reconstruction Party (PRN), held only a handful of seats in the newly elected Congress. The PRN had been hastily organized a year before the elections, after the traditional parties rejected Collor's presidential candidacy. Like most political parties in Brazil, it did not represent any particular ideology or possess a coherent government program. Instead, it represented an individual—Collor—and was less concerned with actual reform than with gaining political power.

When Collor took office in March 1990, inflation had reached a monthly rate of 81 percent. He appointed a relatively unknown economist, Zélia Cardoso de Mello (no relation to the president), as minister of economy, finance, and planning and promised to kill inflation with one "silver bullet"—a new heterodox economic shock program known as the Collor Plan (see box 5-2.) The president also announced plans to open up the Brazilian economy through trade liberalization, privatization of state-owned companies, and a stronger focus on foreign investment.

Facing hyperinflation, Collor and his economic team immediately introduced a new anti-inflation program. With the new plan, 80 percent of all deposits in the overnight market, both transactions and savings accounts, that exceeded the equivalent of $1,300 were frozen for eighteen months and were to receive a return of the prevailing rate equal to inflation plus 6 percent a year. In addition, a new currency was introduced—the cruzeiro—and a once-and-for-all tax on financial transactions was charged on the stock of financial assets, on transactions in gold and stocks, and on withdrawals from savings accounts. There was also an initial price and wage freeze, with subsequent adjustments based on expected inflation, and various types of fiscal incentives were eliminated. Taxes were indexed, administrative measures were introduced to reduce tax evasion, public service prices were increased, the exchange rate was liberalized, various federal government agencies were to be closed, and 360,000 public sector workers were to be dismissed.

The sharp decrease in liquidity, since assets had been frozen, led to a pronounced fall in economic activities. A fear of recession and political pressure from various groups in society led the government to release many blocked financial assets ahead of schedule, but without creating clear rules of the game. The government's effort to reduce public sector workers was constrained by the constitution, which stated that all government employees who were employed for more than five years could not be dismissed. Many of the measures to improve the government's fiscal situation required amendments to the constitution that required a two-thirds vote by Congress; Collor did not have the support to move forward on that front. The program had little popular support in part because it was confusing and in part because it failed so quickly. In Congress there was little support for the program or for Collor, who was treated as an upstart in national politics and, in turn, dealt with the congressional leadership in an off-hand and condescending manner.

The inability to control inflation and the unpopularity of the general goals of the program led to the announcement of Collor II in 1991. It repeated some of the measures of the first plan but emphasized better management of cash flow and a tightening of the budgets of state enterprises. Ministry budgets were frozen. Transfers to the states and municipalities, as mandated in the 1988 constitution, were reduced, while observing the minimum levels required. As it became clear that neither Collor I nor Collor II had killed inflation or dealt with the fiscal imbalances in the budget, the economic team was replaced in May 1991. The new finance minister, Marcílio Marques Moreira, said that there would be no more shock programs while he served as minister. His program was one of relatively orthodox measures to control inflation, continue the privatization of state companies, and oversee the release of the remaining blocked assets from Collor I. But public spending continued, and cash inflows were lower than

expected. Investors remained wary of the unpredictability of the investment climate. Marques Moreira's well-meaning efforts were undermined
by dramatic political events in Brasília in mid-1992.

In May 1992 Collor was accused of involvement in an influence-
peddling scheme. A congressional investigation was launched, and
growing segments of the public turned against the president, who was
impeached and driven from office in December 1992. Collor lost his
political rights for eight years, but they were later restored, and in 2006
he was elected to the federal Senate from his home state of Alagoas.

Itamar Franco and the Origins of the *Real* Plan

Vice President Itamar Franco, a quirky and relatively marginal political
figure, succeeded Collor in office. Long active in politics in his home
state of Minas Gerais, he was serving as a federal senator when chosen
as Collor's vice presidential candidate; no one ever expected him to succeed to the presidency. With no economic experience, Itamar acted errat-
ically, changing finance ministers three times in four months before
moving his foreign minister, Fernando Henrique Cardoso, to the top economic leadership position in May 1993. At the time, Cardoso was known
primarily as a prominent sociologist and writer. He had been exiled by the
military regime, first to Chile and then to France, where he taught at the
Sorbonne. In the early years of the dictatorship, he was an outspoken
opponent of the regime. Upon his return to Brazil after the military
declared an amnesty in August 1979, he was elected to the federal Senate
from his home state of São Paulo. As finance minister, Cardoso called
together a team of young but pragmatic economists who set out to undo
the damage of the last decade. The result was the *Real* Plan.[8] Announced
in December 1993, the program had three elements: the introduction
of an equilibrium budget that Congress approved relatively quickly, a
process of general indexation of prices, and the introduction of a new currency that would be pegged to the U.S. dollar.

In some ways, the *Real* Plan did not look very different from the failed
Cruzado Plan of 1986 (see table 5-1). However, there was at least one
critical difference: the immediate emphasis given to fiscal austerity. A second important component was the decision to call the new approach an
"immediate action plan" to be discussed with Congress and publicly
debated. The centerpiece was a $6 billion cut in government spending that
amounted to 9 percent of federal spending and 2.5 percent of spending at

TABLE 5-1. Overview of Economic Stabilization Plans

Time period	Plan or policy	President	Finance minister
1986 (March)	Cruzado Plan	José Sarney	Dilson Funaro
1986 (November)	Cruzado Plan II	José Sarney	Dilson Funaro
1987 (April)	Bresser Plan	José Sarney	Luiz Bresser-Pereira
1988 (January)	Rice and Beans	José Sarney	Maílson da Nóbrega
1989 (January)	Summer Plan	José Sarney	Maílson da Nóbrega
1990 (March)	Collor Plan	Fernando Collor de Mello	Zélia Cardoso de Mello
1994 (July)	*Real* Plan	Itamar Franco	Fernando Henrique Cardoso

Source: Author's compilation.

all levels of government. Tax collection was tightened, and a new effort was made to resolve the tensions between the federal government and the states and municipalities over transfers from the central budget. Measures were introduced to fight tax evasion. In December 2003 Cardoso proposed to Congress a new stabilization program that hoped to avoid many of the weaknesses of its predecessors. The "proposal" was favorably received by a majority in Congress, who were increasingly convinced that continued inflation would ultimately undermine their political careers. As explained by the economic team, the proposal contained a serious fiscal adjustment and a new indexing system that would lead eventually to a new currency. After much discussion, Congress approved the proposal.

The major fiscal adjustment decisions included an across-the-board tax increase of 5 percent; a new Social Emergency Fund that would receive 15 percent of all tax receipts and would help in making the fiscal adjustment acceptable to the more marginal citizens who needed a temporary support system while the new program was implemented; and spending cuts on government investments, personnel, and state companies to equal about $7 billion. The fund was only a temporary measure, and the government announced long-term plans for constitutional amendments that would transfer to state governments and municipalities responsibilities for health, education, social services, housing, basic sanitation, and irrigation. The amendments to the 1988 constitution would also seek to decrease the automatic transfer of federal tax receipts to state and local governments as mandated by the constitution.

The new indexing system was introduced in February 1994. The economic team identified an "indexer" called the unit of real value (URV) that was tied to the U.S. dollar on a one-to-one basis. Depending on the prevailing rate of inflation, the URV's quotation in the local currency rose

FIGURE 5-1. Percentage Change in GDP and the Consumer Price Index, 1985–96

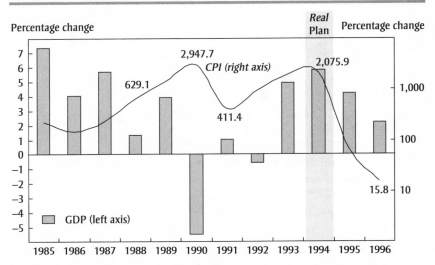

Source: Economist Intelligence Unit, "Brazil Country Finance" (London: EIU, 2009).

daily, accompanying the exchange rate. Official prices, contracts, and taxes were denominated in the URV, and the government team encouraged its use on a voluntary basis by private companies. Gradually an increasing number of prices were stated in URVs, although transactions continued to be carried out in the local currency. As the new plan gained popularity, the economic team decided to introduce a new currency on July 1, 1994. They called it the *real*. Along with the new currency, the government adopted a restrictive monetary policy consisting of a short-term limit on loans to finance exports, a 100 percent reserve requirement on new deposits, and a limit on the expansion of the monetary base.

The implementation of the new plan was gradual and transparent, and its success was almost immediate. Annual inflation quickly fell from four-digit levels in 1994 to less than 100 percent in 1995 and to less than 5 percent in 1998 (see figure 5-1).[9] For the first time in years, Brazilians experienced sustained price stability. GDP growth was strong, averaging 4 percent a year from 1994 to 1997, compared to flat or declining output in the previous five years, and investment climbed above 16 percent of GDP after stagnating for more than a decade.[10]

Nominal salaries also rose, and real salaries were 18.9 percent higher in the first two months of 1995 than a year earlier.[11] As the purchasing power of workers' incomes increased, consumption rose 16.3 percent between the second quarter of 1994 and the second quarter of 1995.[12] Businesses profited as a result. A sample survey of seventy-two enterprises undertaken by the magazine *Exame* found that their profits rose from only $67 million in 1993 to $5.5 billion in 1994 , and the average rate of return rose from 3.1 percent in 1993 to 9.8 percent in 1994.[13]

Based on the *Real* Plan's success, Cardoso resigned as finance minister in April 1994 and declared that he would be a candidate for president that October. He ran with the backing of President Franco and the Brazilian Social Democratic Party (PSDB), a group of former PMDB legislators that he had helped to organize in 1988. He was also supported by the right-leaning Party of the Liberal Front, which supplied a vice presidential candidate for the ticket. Cardoso's PSDB was popular in the more modern and urban southeast of the country, while the PFL represented the more traditional areas in Brazil's north and northeast. A seemingly odd combination, the ticket represented the reality of Brazilian politics. Political parties had multiplied since the return to democracy in 1985, requiring complicated political negotiations at all levels prior to elections. No one party was ever able to win a majority to govern; therefore, regional and local alliances were essential. Many of the new political organizations were personalist in nature and represented local and state political clans or oligarchies.

The other leading presidential candidate in 1994 was Lula, who once again stood for the Workers Party. The party stuck to its antimarket rhetoric, calling for aggressive social reforms and denouncing the *Real* Plan. But given the success of the *Real* Plan, Lula and his party were increasingly seen as part of the past rather than a prescription for the future of the country. As the sustainability of its economic program became increasingly certain, the Cardoso ticket surged in the polls. By July Cardoso was in the lead, propelled by the argument that the PT was against the *Real* Plan and for inflation. In October his ticket won the first round of voting with 54.3 percent of the valid votes cast. Lula placed second. In addition, the PSDB won six governorships, including the states of Minas Gerais, São Paulo, and Rio de Janeiro, which accounted for nearly 60 percent of Brazil's GNP and tax base. The new president took the oath of office on January 1, 1995.

The success of the *Real* Plan and the subsequent election of Fernando Henrique Cardoso constituted a critical juncture in Brazilian history. For the first time, the country had an intelligent, pragmatic leader who understood the importance of both placating the traditional political class and fending off pressure to print money and break the bank. In addition, the success of the *Real* Plan gave Cardoso and his associates the opportunity to move forward with a program to open the economy to international trade and capital movements, as well as widespread liberalization of the economy, and to make it increasingly competitive, laying the groundwork for Brazil's eventual emergence as a BRIC.

6 | The Cardoso Era, 1995–2002

The election of Fernando Henrique Cardoso represented a critical juncture in Brazilian history. For decades Brazil's political leaders had been unable to provide the vision and leadership needed to realize the country's vast potential. Cardoso was the first president who seemed up to the job. As he took office, he was already a star—not just a past foreign and finance minister, but also a well-established academic and writer, an excellent speaker, and an individual with sophisticated experience at the international level. The question was whether or not he could govern a country that had been seeking stability since 1985 (or since 1930, some would say).

Cardoso's Reform Agenda

At the outset of his administration, Cardoso held a relatively strong hand. The *Real* Plan was very popular. Unemployment was low, and the inflation rate was less than 1 percent. The world economy was supportive, with global GDP growth rates around 4 percent, after recovering from the widespread downturn at the beginning of the decade. The parties that had backed Cardoso—the Brazilian Social Democratic Party (PSDB) and the Party of the Liberal Front (PFL)—held a plurality of votes in Congress, although they still needed to negotiate with smaller parties to form a majority. Several key states had elected governors sympathetic to his intended program, although the governors, who were relatively independent power brokers, would still need to be convinced that coop-eration was in their interest.

The broad reform agenda that Cardoso sent to Congress in early 1995 included both old and new elements. One of the administration's top priorities—downsizing the public sector and reducing the number of costly, often inefficient state companies—represented the continuation of a process that had been under way in some form since the late 1970s. The Collor de Mello government had initiated a large-scale program of privatization by announcing the creation of the National Privatization Program in March 1990, and the Franco administration had continued down the same path. Resistance to these efforts was initially high. Each company put up for privatization aroused opposition from different con-stituencies, including unions, consumers, and activists, and organized protests were common. Congress also opposed both the elimination of jobs and the reduction of opportunities to exercise political patronage. However, with the success of each privatization, the process gained sup-port and momentum.

Under the Cardoso administration, the speed of privatization increased, and the program expanded beyond the manufacturing sector (steel, petro-chemicals, fertilizer), which had been its focus during the early 1990s, to include one of the world's largest mining firms (the Rio Doce Valley Company), public utilities (including telecommunications and electricity companies), and firms owned by individual states and municipalities, which were responsible for most of the state-owned enterprise deficit.[1] Altogether, between October 1991 and December 2005, more than 120 state enterprises were sold, generating $87 billion in proceeds, and $18 billion in debt was transferred to the private sector.[2] This revenue stream helped the government to ward off a serious fiscal crisis during Cardoso's first term in office.

Other aspects of the Cardoso program represented a sharper break with the past and required amendments to the constitution. The goal of these measures was to weaken state-held monopolies in critical sectors and introduce private and foreign competition. In the energy sector, the government sought to allow foreign-owned companies to invest in oil extraction and proposed that both foreign and Brazilian companies be allowed to distribute natural gas to households and industry, a task reserved for Petrobras, the state-owned oil giant. It sought to promote competition and modernization in telecommunications by allowing both Brazilian and foreign companies to provide telephone and data transmission services under license from the federal government. Under the 1988 constitution, only Telebrás, the state company, and its subsidiaries were able to grant licenses. Similarly, another proposed amendment allowed foreign companies to compete in coastal shipping, an activity placed off-limits for foreign firms by the constitution.

These reforms—all of which passed—were viewed as revolutionary. At the time, Brazil had a closed, protectionist economy. The Cardoso government called for a gradual opening, more competition, new investment, and transparency in the delivery of vital services. In addition, the government sought to begin the arduous task of fiscal reform by reorganizing the complicated tax system and reforming social security, which had added enormously to the federal deficit over many years. A proposal to reorganize the social security system was introduced in March 1995, but it was quickly buried in committee. Social security benefits were viewed as sacrosanct by employees (especially in the public sector) and their representatives in Congress. Facing entrenched opposition, the administration decided to retreat and leave social security reform for a later date.[3]

Like proposals for social security reform, efforts to overhaul the tax system faced an uphill political battle. In mid-1995 the administration presented a constitutional amendment (which was ultimately adopted) that sought to simplify the taxation system and thereby tighten tax collection and reduce tax evasion, which had grown over the previous decade, causing the government to lose between $40 billion and $60 billion a year.[4] At the same time, it attacked the fiscal problem from the other direction by seeking approval of a Fiscal Responsibility Law (LRF). In hindsight, the LRF was one of the most important initiatives of the Cardoso government. For decades, the fiscal laxity at all levels of government had been a serious Achilles' heel in governing Brazil. All levels of the state bureaucracy overspent and expected the federal government to cover this irresponsible behavior by either printing money or issuing public bonds. Both were sources of inflation and indebtedness. Approved in May 2000, the LRF strengthened fiscal institutions and established a broad framework of fiscal planning, execution, and transparency at the federal, state, and municipal levels. Among other provisions, the LRF required the presentation of fiscal administration reports at four-month intervals, with a detailed account of budget execution and compliance with the LRF provisions. In terms of expenditure, the LRF set ceilings on personnel spending—inclusive of pensions and payments to subcontractors—at 50 percent of federal government spending and 60 percent of state and local government spending. If these limits were breached in any given four-month period, the lapse would need to be redressed within the following eight months. There were strict penalties, including prison terms, for public officials who violated the provision of the law or engaged in other proscribed fiscal actions, as legislated in the Fiscal Crimes Law.

In terms of public debt, the Fiscal Responsibility Law and complementary legislation set a ceiling of 120 percent of current revenue at the national and state levels. If this ceiling were breached, the debt would have to be brought back within the ceiling over the following twelve months, and no form of borrowing would be permitted until that happened. There was also a "golden rule" provision, stating that net borrowing could not exceed the volume of capital spending. Loans between the national, state, and municipal governments were outlawed. The LRF contained two escape clauses that would suspend the application of the debt ceiling. The first escape clause would apply in the case of a Congress-declared state of national calamity or state of siege. The second one would apply in the case of economic recession, defined as a growth rate of less than 1 percent of GDP over a period of one year. In the latter case, the period for redressing a breach in the debt ceiling would be doubled over two years. The escape clauses would also apply to the limits on personnel spending.

While all of these initiatives were welcome, the principal dilemma remained unresolved—the need for deeper structural fiscal reform. Cardoso found it impossible to build a congressional coalition to undertake such painful but necessary reforms as reducing the public sector payroll. Public sector jobs were one of the lifelines of Brazilian politics, and public employees were organized and vocal; thus Congress refused to act. The number of public employees remained very high, and their real wages continued to climb, a problem exacerbated by the decision to raise the minimum wage in 1995. The government also failed in its efforts to reform the civil service pension system. As a result, pension expenditures climbed from 35 to 43 percent of total public sector personnel expenditures between the end of 1992 and the late 1990s.[5]

A similar story could be told about many of the other factors that were contributing to Brazil's fiscal problems, including the previously mentioned deficit in the social security system, the federal government's obligation to transfer substantial financial resources, and the government's need to rescue failed state banks, which had been used for partisan political purposes for decades. In all of these areas, a drastic reduction in federal and state spending was essential. But only Congress could take the required decisions, and it refused to do so.

B O X 6 - 1 . Mexican Peso Crisis: Background

In early 1994 financial conditions began to tighten in some industrial countries. In the United States, for example, short-term interest rates were raised gradually but substantially. Political shocks in Mexico were followed by a fall in capital inflows, a depreciation of the peso to the edge of its intervention band, and a large loss of foreign exchange reserves in April. Despite allowing interest rates on short-term peso-denominated debt to rise, which assisted in momentarily reducing pressures on the peso, credit from the Bank of Mexico to the financial system, and from banks to the private sector, was allowed to expand. The current account deficit widened to 7 percent of GDP. Authorities began replacing a large amount of their outstanding short-term peso-denominated debt with short-term instruments payable in pesos but indexed to the U.S. dollar. After President Ernesto Zedillo was sworn into office in December 1994, there was a large drop in foreign exchange reserves (from $25 billion in early November to $6 billion), and authorities allowed the peso to float. Consequently, the peso depreciated, and by the end of January the currency was worth almost 40 percent less than it had been at the end of November. With Mexico on the brink of default, the United States proposed a package of more than $50 billion from the U.S. Treasury, the International Monetary Fund, the Bank for International Settlements, and private institutions.

Source: Peter Isard, *Globalization and the International Financial System: What's Wrong and What Can Be Done?* (Cambridge University Press, 2005), p. 134.

Moreover, the cause of fiscal reform was weakened by the government's decision to seek an amendment to the constitution to allow the president to run for a second term. This opened a complicated process of providing inducements—some would say bribes—to members of Congress in exchange for their support of the amendment. It finally was approved in June 1997—together with a measure allowing state governors and mayors to run for reelection—at a very high fiscal cost (special interests at the state and local level had to be accommodated; unnecessary projects were funded for local political purposes).

External Shocks Buffet Brazil

In addition to domestic barriers to reform, the Cardoso government also confronted several external shocks that made the task of governing significantly more difficult. The first external shock was the Mexican peso crisis of 1994–95 (see box 6-1).[6] A toxic combination of large capital inflows, a large current account deficit financed by short-term dollar-denominated debt, market liberalization, a weak banking sector, a crawling-band exchange rate, and the perception of political instability brought about an emergency devaluation of the peso in December 1994. As a result, the Mexican economy contracted 20 percent, and the country abandoned its narrow exchange rate band, replacing it with a floating exchange rate.

The crisis threatened the global financial system through the "tequila effect," the pressure applied to currencies in Latin America and East Asia following the crash. Like many of its neighbors, Brazil was vulnerable to contagion from the crisis, due to its overvalued currency, weak financial position, and large current account deficit. But Brazilian authorities responded effectively by moving quickly to devalue the *real*. In March 1995 the central bank adopted a crawling band, which increased the flexibility of the exchange rate regime while maintaining an anchor for inflationary expectations. The exchange rate depreciated 13.9 percent in 1995, 7.1 percent in 1996, 7.3 percent in 1997, and 8.3 percent in 1998. The decision was also taken to support the *real* by raising interest rates. Starting in March 1995, real borrowing rates by banks were kept at an annualized rate of 25 to 30 percent, and real lending rates rose as high as 60 to 70 percent on an annualized basis.[7]

As a result of these policies, inflation remained under control from 1995 to 1998, despite the government's inability to implement fiscal reform. However, the federal government's primary balance (which excludes interest payments on public debt) moved from surplus in 1994 to deficit in 1998. The principal reason was the failure to limit the rise in expenditures at all levels of government, particularly for new public sector employees (see figure 6-1). The operational budget balance (which includes interest payments, but not the nominal marking up of the stock of debt during the era of high inflation) also deteriorated over this period, creating the need for additional government borrowing. By the end of 1999, Brazil's public debt amounted to almost half of the annual GDP. This high debt level discouraged economic growth by putting upward pressure on interest rates and absorbed budgetary resources from other essential areas, including education, health care, and public infrastructure.[8]

The strategy also created a persistent current account deficit. The deficit was financed through inflows of foreign capital and increased domestic and foreign debt. As the current account deficit grew, the interest rate dif-

FIGURE 6-1. **Primary and Operational Budget Balance as a Percentage of GDP, 1989–99**

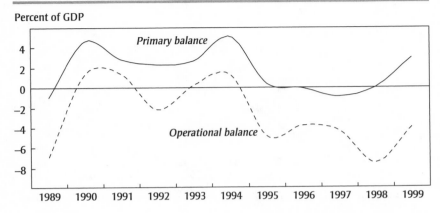

Percent of GDP

Source: Lincoln Gordon, *Brazil's Second Chance: En Route toward the First World* (Brookings Institution Press, 2001), p.186.

ferentials in favor of the Brazilian market had to rise, to continue to attract inflows of foreign capital. Higher interest rates, however, reduced economic activity, increased the costs of servicing outstanding debt payments, and caused a rapid expansion in the ratio of public debt to GDP (see figure 6-2). Moreover, as capital inflows increased, so did the level of external indebtedness, making the country more vulnerable to external shocks.

In the wake of the Mexican peso crisis, Brazil benefited from very positive global financial trends, including interest rates favorable to emerging markets (global interest rates were low) and domestic macroeconomic conditions attractive to foreign capital flows. International reserves were in the range of $55 billion to $60 billion, and interest rates were gradually declining.[9] But the country's economic health remained fragile, as the outbreak of the Asian financial crisis in 1997 and the Russian collapse in 1998 made dramatically clear. The Asian financial crisis began when the government of Thailand devalued the baht on July 2, 1997, allowing the currency to float. The decision to devalue quickly spread to the region and then to emerging markets around the world. Brazil was potentially vulnerable, given the weak links in the *Real* Plan: an overvalued currency and a growing current account deficit. Brazil shared these deficiencies with many emerging-market economies that relied on overvalued currencies in order to promote industrial development and stabilize prices at the same

FIGURE 6-2. Ratio of Net Public Debt to GDP, 1995–2002

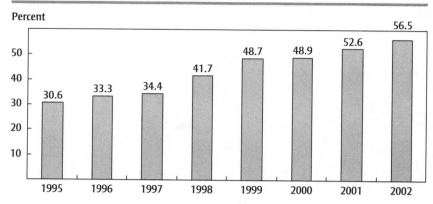

Source: International Monetary Fund, *The IMF and Recent Capital Account Crises: Indonesia, Korea, and Brazil* (Washington: IMF, 2003), p. 21.

time. In the wake of the Asian financial crisis, nearly $8 billion of Brazil's foreign exchange reserves drained away in October 1997. Authorities responded by raising interest rates from 19 to 43 percent and tightening fiscal policy, which stopped the outflow of reserves and induced a resumption of capital inflows.[10] International reserves rose steadily from November 1997 to April 1998, reaching a record high of $75 billion, while interest rates fell each month until by August they were lower than before the crisis.[11]

Nevertheless, in the summer of 1998, market pressures on Brazil intensified following Russia's default on its external debt and the subsequent devaluation of the ruble. The situation was made more difficult with the crisis surrounding a major U.S. investment fund, Long-Term Capital Management, which led to a sharp decrease in liquidity in international capital markets.[12] Suddenly, international capital was not readily available, worsening Brazil's fiscal plight. The central bank doubled interest rates in early September to 42 percent, while the Cardoso administration promised to tackle fiscal deficits, but both measures failed to stem capital outflows.[13] Reserves plummeted from $75 billion in August 1998 to less than $35 billion in January 1999 (see figure 6-3).[14] Portfolio investment flows became negative as investors took their money home. Interest rates were raised to a new high to encourage investors to remain in Brazil, reaching levels of close to 50 percent in annualized real terms in September 1998.[15]

FIGURE 6-3. Current Account Balance, International Reserves, and External Debt (Yearly Averages), 1995–2002

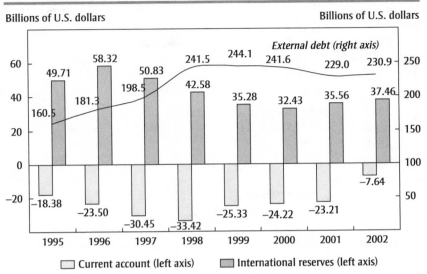

Source: Economist Intelligence Unit, "Brazil Country Finance" (London: EIU, 2009).

Cardoso's Second Term

Amid the economic chaos, Cardoso won a second term as president in October 1998, again defeating Lula on the Workers Party (PT) ticket. Cardoso was elected in the first round with 53.1 percent of the votes cast; Lula received 31.7 percent. But the election for the Chamber of Deputies, critical for approving legislation submitted by the president, demonstrated the challenge of building a stable coalition. The largest number of votes went to Cardoso's party, 17.5 percent; the allied PFL polled 17.3 percent; the ubiquitous Brazilian Democratic Movement Party (PMDB) took 15.2 percent; and the PT of Lula received 13.2 percent of the vote. The rest were spread across ten or eleven small regional or personalist parties. While a majority president, Cardoso would face the arduous task of assembling a support group through bargaining and cajoling over every piece of draft legislation. Senate results were similar. The PSDB received 18.8 percent; the PMDB, 17.9 percent; the PT, 15.9 percent; and the PFL, 15.6 percent. While votes in the Senate were more clustered, each vote required the construction of a majority.

State governorship elections resulted in stronger support for Cardoso. Of the twenty-seven governors elected in 1998, nineteen belonged, more or less, to the Cardoso coalition. Cardoso scored an important political victory with the reelection of Mário Covas as governor of São Paulo, Brazil's richest state and the center of the country's financial and industrial sectors. Covas defeated Paulo Maluf of the right-wing Brazilian Progressive Party (PPB). Maluf was viewed by many as a spendthrift populist whose election would have severely hampered the efforts to achieve fiscal reform proposed by Cardoso. But opposition candidates won in the important states of Minas Gerais, Rio de Janeiro, and Rio Grande do Sul.

In large part, Cardoso's victory was due to the voters' perception that the economy had been well managed in his first term, despite the dark clouds gathered on the horizon. Under Cardoso's leadership, inflation had fallen to single digits, annual growth had been above 3 percent on average, annual private consumption had risen around 5 percent on average in nominal terms, and inward direct investment flows had skyrocketed from well under $5 billion to $30 billion between 1998 and 2002. Immediately following his victory, the president sought to capitalize on his popularity by pressuring Congress to pass amendments to the constitution that would raise taxes on retirees' pension contributions and increase and make permanent a special tax on financial transactions. Both measures were intended to bolster the government's fiscal position. But the government was unable to guide its proposals through the cumbersome amendment process, which required each of the two houses of Congress to vote twice to approve an amendment, with a three-fifths majority in favor each time.[16]

Meanwhile, the international financial community sought a "firewall" to protect the Brazilian economy. In light of the Russian default and the Asian financial crisis, there were expectations that Brazil might default because of its controversial policy of maintaining its crawling peg, despite a widely held perception in the markets that the *real* was substantially overvalued. According to the International Monetary Fund (IMF), however, Brazilians thought that any overvaluation was modest and feared that abandoning the anchor would reignite inflation.[17]

Strongly supported by the Clinton administration, the IMF and the World Bank put together a package of $41.5 billion in November 1998 in an effort to support the *real*. The package allowed Brazil to maintain its existing exchange rate regime but required the government to run a substantial primary fiscal surplus for the next three years (1999–2001).

The primary goal of this program was to stabilize the ratio of net public debt to GDP at 47 percent by 2000 and to bring it down thereafter.[18]

Congress reluctantly supported the first set of fiscal adjustment measures demanded under the IMF plan, including a decrease from 80 to 60 percent in the share of its revenue that the federal government transferred to the states and a fine on states and municipalities that spent more than 60 percent of net revenue on their payroll bills.[19] In December, however, it rejected the government's proposals for social security reform, which would have increased taxes on higher-paid civil service pensioners.[20] This setback was viewed very negatively by investors, and capital outflows accelerated at the end of the year. But the final blow to efforts to protect the currency was Governor Itamar Franco's decision in January 1999 to declare a moratorium on payments on the debt owed by the state of Minas Gerais. This decision by the former president was seen by many as "payback" against Cardoso, whom Franco resented for having taken the lion's share of credit for the *Real* Plan.

By mid-January 1999 the financial authorities conceded defeat. The government allowed the exchange rate to float. Over the next two months, the value of the *real* fell 40 percent. But the decision to appoint Armínio Fraga, an experienced Wall Street investment banker, as central bank governor quickly restored credibility to the institution and bolstered investor confidence in the medium-term outlook for the economy. Fraga was able to begin reducing interest rates from their high of 45 percent in small increments, which helped to restore confidence in the management of the economy.

In addition, like its counterparts in several other Latin American countries, the central bank adopted an inflation targeting strategy with its principal goal as the attainment and maintenance of a certain level of inflation (see box 6-2). The simplicity of this approach, which made it easy to communicate to the public, was one of its advantages. Moreover, in contrast to an exchange rate peg, this strategy allowed "monetary policy to focus on domestic considerations and to respond flexibly to the domestic economy."[21]

At the same time, the Cardoso team took various measures to produce the primary budget surplus required by the IMF. The government agreed to achieve a primary budget surplus of 3.1 percent of GDP. Congress passed legislation to raise taxes for higher-income earners, but efforts to do the same for active public sector employees and to impose taxes on inactive public workers were declared unconstitutional. Public

---

BOX 6-2. Tracking Brazil's Exchange Rate since the *Real* Plan

Fixed exchange rate (1994–95)
—The *real* is created and fixed to the U.S. dollar at one-to-one.
—Responsible monetary policy is pegged to a credible currency.
—Price stability is established, and vulnerability of the exchange rate to volatile market conditions is eliminated.

Crawling band (1995–99)
—The *real* is allowed to appreciate or depreciate against the U.S. dollar within a predetermined range.

Floating exchange rate (1999–present)
—The *real* is no longer fixed against another base currency.
—The value of the *real* is determined by the market.
—Monetary policy is free to focus on policy goals other than maintaining an agreed exchange rate.

The basics of inflation targeting (1999–present)
—Medium-term numerical targets for inflation are publicly announced.
—Commitment to stability becomes the primary goal of monetary policy.
—An all-inclusive strategy is adopted that includes many variables in deciding the setting of policy instruments.
—A commitment is made to increased transparency and communication to ensure that the public understands the strategy and the bank's policies.
—The central bank assumes more accountability in its pursuit of the target.

---

expectations for investment in education, wages, and job creation could not be met given the tight budget situation; thus the government resorted to a series of other measures to cut expenditures and raise taxes. In combination with high interest rates, these measures limited economic growth (see figure 6-4).

However, following the devaluation and the seeming inability of the government to reinitiate a reform agenda, the Cardoso administration lost momentum. The president's popularity never recovered, and it was apparent that the public was looking forward to a new government even though the transition was somewhat distant in the future. As hesitant efforts to reinitiate structural reforms stalled in Congress, it became clear that political attention had turned to the next national election at the end of 2002.

FIGURE 6-4. Percentage Change in GDP and the Consumer Price Index, 1995–2002

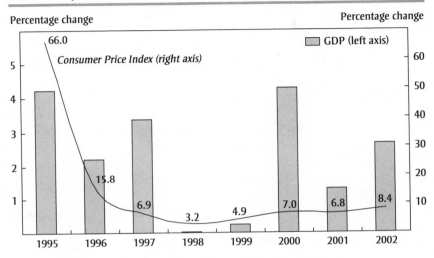

Source: Economist Intelligence Unit, "Brazil Country Finance" (London: EIU, 2009).

If any doubt remained about the weakness of the Cardoso regime, it disappeared when a widespread power shortage in 2001 caused another sharp drop in the government's popularity. For many, this episode sealed the fate of the PSDB-PFL alliance.

Enter Lula and the Beginning of a New Era

The presidential campaign of 2002 (which began in 2001) saw the juxtaposition of two very different candidates. José Serra, a former minister of health and close colleague of President Cardoso, secured the PSDB-PFL nomination; Lula was selected, for the fourth time, as the leader of the PT coalition. This time Lula and the PT sensed that their time had come.

Serra's campaign was handicapped by his links to Cardoso and the highly unpopular "Washington consensus," which the outgoing government had embraced. The Washington consensus, a strategy for economic modernization formulated in the 1980s, called for reducing fiscal imbalances and inflation, opening the economy to international trade, undertaking deregulation, developing domestic capital markets, and privatizing state-owned enterprises.[22] As countries implemented some combination of these policies in the first half of the 1990s, they achieved some success in controlling inflation and generating growth.[23] But the consensus did not address job creation, poverty reduction, or investment in health and education. Nor did it address such important areas as improving institutional transparency and accountability in the region's judicial systems. Thus by the end of the decade there was widespread public discontent with government policies that sought to fix the economy, but not civil society.

The election of Hugo Chávez in Venezuela in 1998 signaled a sharp rejection of the policies suggested by the consensus, which were strongly supported by the United States and the multilateral agencies in Washington. This antipathy spread throughout the region, and by 2001–02, Brazilians too were ready for new policies and for new people to take charge. Much of what the Cardoso regime had accomplished was overlooked or forgotten, leaving the stage open for the PT.

While Serra, as the candidate of the governing coalition, was forced to defend the general reform commitment of the past eight years, Lula lashed out at the Cardoso record: "Lula campaigned in 2002 explicitly against the market-oriented neoliberal economic reforms embraced by his predecessor. . . . His opposition to these market-oriented reforms resonated among Brazilians, many of whom had become disenchanted with the course of economic policy under Cardoso."[24] Yet Lula signaled that he had a pragmatic side as well. In June the candidate issued his now famous "*carta ao povo brasileiro*" (letter to the Brazilian people). Allegedly released without party approval, the letter stated unequivocally that Lula's government would honor all of Brazil's debts, contracts, and other outstanding financial obligations. The document committed the new administration to social justice and to poverty reduction, but it did so in the context of moderate fiscal policies.

Despite this change of heart, the possibility of a PT victory produced growing agitation in international financial markets through the summer of 2002. With hindsight, it is clear that key market analysts were looking back at the previous three campaigns and the rhetoric of the "old" PT. As the campaign progressed, political risk indicators soared.[25] Concern grew among international investors that the rules of the game were going to change dramatically and not in their favor. The greatest risk, from the perspective of international investors, was a default on the public debt.

President Cardoso was acutely aware of the danger both to his legacy and to the financial stability of the country. He met with all of the candidates, including minor party representatives, in August and asked them to

BOX 6-3. The Argentine Default: Background

In 1991 Argentina established a currency board that mandated the convertibility of one peso to one dollar at a fixed peg. While the currency board was successful in reducing inflation to single digits by the end of 1994, several factors contributed to the vulnerability of Argentina's economy. As in Brazil, these included the appreciation of the dollar to which the peso was pegged, leading to an overvalued real exchange rate, an increasing current account deficit, and rising external debt. As government revenues were increasing less than expenditures, the government borrowed in the international financial markets. If interest rates remain stable, the government can often roll over existing debt with further borrowing. But when lenders decide that the ability "to pay" or service or repay the debt is unlikely, lending stops. As the various financial crises unfolded in 1997–99—Asia, Russia, and Brazil—Argentina's expanding debt profile looked increasingly unmanageable. Finally, in December 2001, the government of President Fernando de la Rúa was driven from office after widespread riots protesting the collapsing economy. His successor suspended payment of the government debt. Congress ended the convertibility system in early January 2002. After suffering increased capital outflows and a deepening of the debt crisis as a result of the 1998 Russian default and the 1999 Brazilian devaluation of the *real*, and despite various efforts to stave off the crisis by increasing taxes, monetizing and swapping debt, and instituting capital controls, in December 2001 Argentina suspended payments on external debt and abandoned the dollar peg. In 2002 real GDP plummeted almost 11 percent, unemployment surpassed 20 percent, inflation averaged about 40 percent, and the public debt ratio increased to about 135 percent by year end.

endorse publicly his government's fiscal policies and to guarantee that they would remain in place no matter who won the race in October. The key issue at stake was a $30 billion loan package, aimed at stabilizing the economy, that the Cardoso team had negotiated with the IMF. With varying degrees of reluctance, all of the candidates (with the exception of a minor contender who was in last place in the polls) did so, but often with disclaimers. Nonetheless, the financial press continued to speculate about a default, pointing to the disastrous default in neighboring Argentina the prior year (see box 6-3). Citing the risk of default, some investment banks downgraded Brazilian bonds to the "underweight category."

As the situation worsened, it became increasingly clear to Lula and his advisers that what separated them from victory was the danger of a shift in public opinion. Most Brazilians understood, if only vaguely, that external events were increasingly relevant to their economic and social welfare. Many moderate voters, disenchanted with Cardoso, seemed prepared to give Lula a chance, but an international scare might be enough to drive them back to the perceived safety of the ruling coalition. To avoid losing these voters' support, Lula took the risk of marginalizing the radical wing of the party. He publicly recognized the seriousness of the situation and focused on projecting an image of probity and responsibility. When Brazilians went to the polls in October 2002, this strategy paid off—in a two-round contest, Lula won with 61.43 percent of the vote compared to Serra's 38.57 percent.[26]

Immediately following their victory, Lula and his team moved quickly to establish their bona fides. The transition team announced that, upon taking office in January 2003, the new government would not only respect the primary surplus of 3.75 percent, but elevate it to 4.25 percent. Indeed, the surplus reached 4.7 percent of GDP in December 2004. Equally important, Lula appointed a well-known international financial figure and member of the PSDB, Henrique Meirelles, as central bank president. Other nominations included the appointment of Finance Minister Antônio Palocci, who quickly became the public face of the government's steady hand in dealing with fiscal issues that reassured markets.[27]

Post Mortem

In hindsight, it is clear that the Cardoso administration began several important programs. The president acknowledged racism as a national problem, which had been overlooked for centuries.[28] He initiated a School Grant (Bolsa Escola) program that paid poor families a monthly stipend to keep their children in school.[29] This was the first of a series of conditional cash transfer programs that would become a hallmark of the next government. Efforts were made to spur land reform. And in a highly publicized struggle with international drug companies, the government created an innovative domestic program to combat acquired immunodeficiency syndrome (AIDS). Finally, Cardoso initiated an important process of raising the country's international standing.[30] All of these undertakings had merit. But in the end, Cardoso's politics relied on the traditional regional bosses that he reluctantly found necessary to make the system work. Time and again, the government had to turn to the established power brokers to approve legislation. This, perhaps unfairly, put him in the political corner of the "old" Brazil.

It is probably fair to say that the Cardoso government did as much as it could during its eight years in power to move Brazil forward. But the government was confronted with an unpleasant reality. To preserve international capital flows and secure the stability of the currency, the authorities were forced to maintain very high real interest rates and to limit public spending. The Cardoso administration also introduced new taxes that increased the burden of an already inefficient tax system in order to generate new government revenues. High interest rates resulted in low inflation but increased the cost of public sector debt and depressed business investment. The new taxes increased government revenues, but at the cost of discouraging formal sector employment and weakening domestic business investment.

A recent review of the Cardoso presidency concludes, "In essence, deficit management and inflation fighting trumped all other considerations, as unemployment increased, consumption declined, the *real* devalued sharply (further hurting consumers' purchasing power), and growth progressed at an anemic average rate of 2.1 percent over the 1999–2002 period (only 1.3 percent if 2000 is excluded)."[31] This weak economic performance led a list of grievances held by average Brazilians that included rising crime in urban centers, a lack of real progress on land reform, corruption scandals, and the 2001 energy crisis. Despite the best of intentions, the Cardoso administration limped to an end in 2002. It would take the new government of Lula and the PT to initiate a new round of reforms after 2002 that would finally transform Brazil into a modern nation.

Lula's Brazil

Lula's Brazil began to come of age as the concept of Brazil, Russia, India, and China (the BRICs) as the future movers and shakers of the global economy took off. Ten months after Lula assumed office on January 1, 2003, Goldman Sachs issued a paper reaffirming the upbeat mood captured by the 2001 report that coined the term. A third paper issued in December 2005, three-quarters of the way through Lula's first term, was even more optimistic: "Since we began writing on the BRICs," the Goldman analysts noted, "each country has grown more strongly than our initial projections. Our updated forecasts suggest the BRICs can realize the 'dream' more quickly than we thought in 2003."[1]

Four years later, as Lula's second and final term drew near its end, Brazil had made impressive strides. Inflation was under control, growth was strong, and the government had taken advantage of the country's large balance-of-payments surpluses to pay down its external debt. In recognition of these accomplishments, international credit-rating agencies had promoted Brazil's sovereign debt to investment-grade status. Brazil had also emerged as a leader in the energy sector, and it was taken for granted that Brazil's president would be included in nearly all important international meetings, a significant departure from the practice of years past.

In short, something had changed in Brazil since the opening of the century. Was it due to luck? Careful planning? Or is Brazil's rise best explained by one of Lula's favorite sayings, "God is a Brazilian"?

TABLE 7-1. Brazil's Leading Economic Indicators, 2002

Indicator	Measure
GDP growth (annual percentage change)	2.66
Inflation (annual percentage change)	8.45
Unemployment rate (percent)	11.68
Total international reserves (billions of U.S. dollars)	37.84
Stock of inward foreign direct investment (billions of U.S. dollars)	100.85
Stock of outward foreign direct investment (billions of U.S. dollars)	54.42
Current account balance (percent of GDP)	−1.51
Total external debt (percent of GDP)	45.65
Public debt (percent of GDP)	59.62
Primary balance (percent of GDP)	3.55
Net debt (percent of GDP)	38.17

Source: Economist Intelligence Unit, "Brazil Country Finance" (London: EIU, 2009).

Lula's Inheritance

When Lula took office in early 2003, Brazil's economic situation was delicate (see table 7-1). Growth was sluggish, Brazil's foreign reserves had fallen below $40 billion, and its external debt amounted to more than 45 percent of the country's GDP. To make things worse, 42 percent of the public debt was denominated in dollars, and by October 2002, the *real* had lost more than 40 percent of its value against the U.S. dollar.[2] Equally important, the international environment was unforgiving. Investors had not yet recovered from the dramatic collapse of the Argentine economy in 2001–02, and many observers expressed concern that Brazil might follow the same path. For example, the *Financial Times* argued that Brazil "can either follow Chile and Mexico in undergoing fundamental political change that reinforces rather than disrupts maturing economic institutions—a path that social democratic governments chose with success in Europe. Or it can embark on the road that Argentina and, increasingly, Venezuela find themselves on—one where political instability undermines the institutions that are needed to anchor growth and poverty reduction."[3] In the second half of 2002 concern increased dramatically, reflecting the fear among money managers and investors that a Lula victory would result in mismanagement of the economy and even a default on Brazil's debt.

To calm such fears, Lula's team took the key decision to reaffirm and strengthen the government's commitment to maintaining fiscal responsibility and a budget surplus. This decision was facilitated by both the growing moderation within the Workers Party (PT) and the move to the center by Brazil's other political parties. Rather than continue to battle the once firmly leftist PT, the conservative parties in Congress allied with Lula to support "an economic agenda so orthodox that his presidency was dubbed 'Cardoso's third term.' "[4] The government tightly controlled expenditures, and revenues rose sharply as a result of greater enforcement and collection. Tax income increased in 2003–04, reaching 36 percent of GDP by 2004. Led by Antônio Palocci (finance minister) and Henrique Meirelles (central bank president and former president of BankBoston in the United States), economic policymakers kept interest rates high and maintained continuity with the inflation-targeting policy that had been implemented in the wake of the January 1999 maxi-devaluation. Officials believed that by committing itself to achieving specific inflation targets, the central bank played an important role in coordinating expectations and reducing inflationary pressures.[5]

The October 2003 Goldman Sachs report endorsed these policy decisions and predicted that, given policy continuity and continued reform, Brazil's GDP growth rate would average 3.6 percent over the next fifty years. While lower than the estimates for India and China, it would be sufficient to overtake the GDP of Italy by 2025, France by 2031, and the United Kingdom and Germany by 2036.[6] However, the Goldman analysts also warned, "More needs to be done to unlock sustained higher growth in Brazil than is the case elsewhere, and our convergence assumptions for Brazil . . . may still prove too optimistic without deeper structural reforms."[7] The report recognized the importance of macroeconomic stabilization—the early focus of the Lula government—as a precondition for reform. But it also called on the government to open up the economy to more trade, to increase investment and saving, which significantly lagged the rates achieved in Asia, and to reduce public and foreign debt, which remained much higher in Brazil than in the other BRICs.

Addressing Structural Challenges

Lula and his economic team were acutely aware of the need for reform. In December 2003 the government achieved a major success when both houses of Congress approved a major change in the social security system, which had been recognized for decades as a leading cause of Brazil's fiscal vulnerability (a few years later it would become clear that the success of the legislation was linked to payments to members of Congress in return for support of the PT bill). Although social security benefited only a few million public servants and their dependents, it absorbed an ever-greater share of the federal budget. (In contrast, the government pension program for private sector workers distributed far fewer resources to a much larger group of clients—almost 20 million individuals.) The Cardoso administration had tried valiantly to reform the system, but its efforts had been defeated by threatened beneficiaries, who mounted a powerful lobbying campaign in Congress.

Lula's reforms raised the minimum retirement age for all civil servants and required retired civil servants to contribute to the social security system if their income exceeded a minimum amount. Among other cost-cutting measures, it limited the pension benefits paid to widows and orphans of civil servants and capped civil servants' wages and retirement earnings. In addition, the law set a cap on pensions paid to private sector retirees. These changes represented an important breakthrough both regarding Lula's ability to convince Congress to support his agenda and as a demonstration that structural reform was feasible in twenty-first-century Brazil.

Also in December 2003 Lula's administration succeeded in revising the tax code. State-based taxes were unified, reducing the number of tax rates from forty-four state taxes to five national rates.[8] The financial transactions tax (a federal tax on financial transactions popularly known as the "check tax"), which had been temporary, was made permanent. Other changes helped to rationalize the "cascading" tax system, which taxed inputs repeatedly at different stages of a good's production, increasing taxes, prices, tax evasion, and barriers to economic growth. While a great deal more must be done to rationalize what is a chaotic system of taxation, the ability of the government to begin the process—again in contrast to the unsuccessful efforts of its predecessors—was noted abroad by investors and the rating agencies.

Equally important, the Lula government implemented some of the most important social reforms in the history of Brazil by building on a small number of initiatives inherited from the Cardoso administration. After some administrative missteps, in October 2003 the government created the Bolsa Família (Family Basket) program, which aims to increase the income of poor families by making cash transfers conditional on behavior such as children's school attendance.[9] The four subprograms of Bolsa Família provide educational stipends, maternal

FIGURE 7-1. Percentage of the Population Living in Poverty and Extreme Poverty, Gini Coefficient, 1990–2007

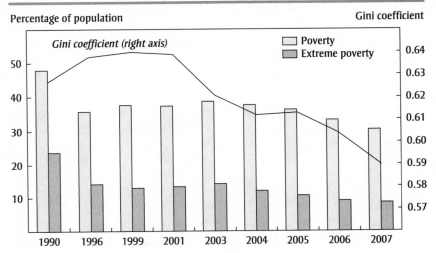

Source: ECLAC CEPALSTAT, Social Indicators and Statistics, Poverty, Brazil.
Note: Poverty is measured as living on $60 a month. Extreme poverty is measured as living on less than $30 a month. The Gini coefficient is a measure of income inequality; a low value indicates a more equal distribution, with 0 being perfect equality and 1 being perfect inequality.

nutrition, food supplements, and a domestic gas subsidy. In 2009 the program reached almost 11 million Brazilians, more than two-thirds of whom earned less than R$60 (about $33) a month.[10] While there has been no systematic evaluation of Bolsa Família's success, the program has been partially credited with a decline in extreme poverty, slight improvements in income inequality, and higher school enrollment among young children (see figure 7-1).[11] And it has done so at the relatively low cost of 2.5 percent of all government expenditures (0.5 percent of GDP).[12] Nonetheless, poverty remains an enormous challenge for Brazil. As one commentator notes, "Inadequate employment, political access, and protection from violence mean that the poor and uneducated do not enjoy the full benefits of citizenship. Democracy cannot deepen without addressing the enormous inequality that undermines the quality of citizenship for the poor."[13]

The education deficit was also a major target of the Lula administration. To improve both access to and quality of education, the government renamed and enlarged Fundef, the Cardoso government's program to supplement local funding for teachers' salaries and schools in poor districts. However, Brazil still lags many of its international competitors, to the detriment of its economy.[14] As the *Economist* reported recently,

> In the OECD's [Organization of Economic Cooperation and Development's] worldwide test of pupils' abilities in reading, math, and science, Brazil is near the bottom of the class. Until the 1970s South Korea was about as prosperous as Brazil, but, helped by its superior school system, it has leapt ahead and now has around four times the national income per head. World domination, even the friendly and non-confrontational sort Brazil seeks, will not come to a place where 45 percent of the heads of poor families have less than a year's schooling.[15]

The Results of Lula's First Term

Lula's economic and social reforms drew international attention and approval. GDP growth rose from only 1.15 percent in 2003 to 5.71 percent in 2004, the strongest expansion since 1996, led by an industrial expansion of 7.89 percent. To control inflationary pressures, driven by the combination of supply-side constraints and surging demand, the government tightly controlled the growth of the money supply beginning in the second half of 2004.[16] By the end of the first half of the Lula government, the fiscal accounts were viewed positively and the overall management of the economy was given high points by both investors and multilateral organizations. The balance of payments improved steadily. The trade surplus increased from $2.6 billion in 2001 to $46.1 billion in 2006, due largely to strong export growth (see figure 7-2). The current account moved from a deficit to a surplus in 2003, reaching $13.5 billion in 2006. As a result of the economy's healthy performance and future prospects, in early 2005 the government decided not to renew its stand-by agreement with the International Monetary Fund (IMF).

However, just as the government appeared to have reached a high level of perceived and actual success, a major scandal involving many of the key figures in the PT erupted. The issue concerned what might be considered a Brazilian "tradition" of buying votes in Congress to gain approval for pending legislation. Despite a general tendency to believe that the PT was above that sort of behavior, in 2006 a congressional fact-finding investigation established a paper trail that led to the resignation of most of Lula's principal advisers and collaborators. The president was not implicated,

FIGURE 7-2. Exports, Imports, and Trade Balance, 2002–08

Billions of U.S. dollars

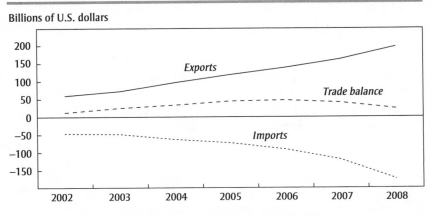

Source: Economist Intelligence Unit, "Brazil Country Finance" (London: EIU, 2009).

which led many to refer to him as the "Teflon president"—no matter how bad things were for PT leaders, he was viewed as blameless.

Some observers argue that the *mensalão* scandal (which involved monthly payments to members of Congress) and the departure of Lula's early coterie of supporters actually liberated the president. Having consolidated his leadership, he was free to pursue a more vigorous personal agenda that included a greater emphasis on international travel and diplomacy. Unscathed by the congressional scandals and aided in great measure by the popularity of the Bolsa Família program, Lula won a second term in office at the end of 2006. However, the voters who returned him to office were not the same group that had elected him in 2002.[17] Lula's strength initially lay in the PT's traditional base: better educated and higher-income voters in the relatively urban and industrial states of Brazil's south and southeast. But in 2006 these voters favored the opposition candidate Geraldo Alckmin of the Brazilian Social Democratic Party (PSDB).[18] Lula owed his victory to the support of Brazil's poor. Between 60 and 85 percent of votes from the impoverished north and northeast of the country went to him.[19] However, their support did not extend to the PT, which lost seats in Congress.

The results of the 2006 general election are more complicated once party voting is considered. Lula did not win in the first round: he received 48.6 percent against his main rival, the PSDB candidate, Geraldo Alckmin, the governor of São Paulo, who received 37.5 percent. Lula would go on to defeat Alckmin, an honest but uninspiring candidate, in the second round, taking 60.8 percent of the vote compared to 39.1 percent for the governor. Analysts argue that the four television debates held between the first and second round of the elections were instrumental in the PT victory. Lula argued that Alckmin would reduce or cancel the Bolsa Família program. The president also questioned the privatization of state companies carried out under Cardoso. He alleged that some of the privatizations were unnecessary and that the state companies were sold for sums much lower than their true market value.

Once again, the congressional vote splintered. In the Chamber of Deputies, the PT carried 15 percent of the vote; the Brazilian Democratic Movement Party (PMDB), 14.6 percent; the PSDB, 13.6 percent; and the Democrats (Dems—formerly the Party of the Liberal Front), 10.9 percent. The rest of the seats were divided among twenty-five smaller parties. The Senate results were similar. The Dems took 25.7 percent; the PT, 19.2 percent; and the PSDB, 12.5 percent. Lula, like his predecessors, faced formidable obstacles in building a supportive coalition.

Lula's Second Term: Continued Improvements

Brazil's economy continued to expand in Lula's second term. GDP growth was 6.1 percent in 2007 and roughly 5 percent in 2008 (see table 7-2). Brazilian exports tripled on rising world demand for soybeans, iron ore, beef, and cars. Once the world's largest emerging-market debtor, Brazil became a net foreign creditor for the first time in January 2008, as international reserves swelled to a record $180.3 billion by the end of 2007 from $49.3 billion in 2003.

These efforts were crowned later that year with the elevation of Brazil's debt to investment-grade status. A major sign of financial stability and consolidation, the investment-grade rating gave Brazil access to a larger and more diverse set of institutional investors who were precluded from investing in countries with lower ratings. It also lowered the country's cost of borrowing and more broadly signaled a reduction in investment risk.

After years of speculation in financial circles about the possibility of a breakthrough for Brazil, on April 30, 2008, Standard and Poor's was the first rating agency to designate Brazil as one of fourteen sovereign states

TABLE 7-2. Brazil's Leading Economic Indicators, 2003–09

Indicator (unit)	2003	2004	2005	2006	2007	2008	2009
Change in GDP (percentage real change per year)	1.177	5.686	3.144	3.944	6.058	5.133	-0.300
Change in consumer prices (average percentage change per year)	14.715	6.597	6.870	4.184	3.641	5.679	4.900
Real exchange rate (consumer-price-index-based, annual percentage change)	-0.0200	0.0434	0.2343	0.1280	0.0829	0.0422	-0.0020
Recorded unemployment (percent)	12.317	11.475	9.825	9.975	9.292	7.892	7.80
International reserves (billions of U.S. dollars)	49.297	52.935	53.799	85.839	180.334	193.784	240.527
Stock of inward foreign direct investment (billions of U.S. dollars)	133	161	196	214	249	294	318
Stock of outward foreign direct investment (billions of U.S. dollars)	55	69	72	100	107	128	123
Current account balance (percent of GDP)	0.756	1.760	1.586	1.253	0.113	-1.721	-1.000
Total debt (percent of GDP)	42.521	33.079	21.257	17.770	17.381	16.000	18.400
Public debt (percent of GDP)	53.716	49.292	46.687	45.040	42.032	38.800	45.300
Primary balance (percent of GDP)	3.893	4.178	4.355	3.804	3.818	3.9	1.2
Net debt (percent of GDP)	33.6	25.1	15.2	9.9	4.2	4.1	2.7

Source: Economist Intelligence Unit, Country Finance, Brazil.

a. Estimated figures are italicized.

with an investment-grade rating (BBB or higher) for its foreign currency debt.[20] The report explained,

> The upgrades reflect the maturation of Brazil's institutions and policy framework, as evidenced by the easing of fiscal and external debt burdens and improved trend growth projects. While net general government debt remains higher than that in many "BBB" peers, a fairly predictable track record of pragmatic fiscal and debt management policies mitigates this risk. The country's external debt net of liquid external assets has declined dramatically, with net debt amounting to a projected 3 percent of current account receipts (CAR) in 2008 from in excess of 100 percent of CAR as recently as 2004.[21]

The agency emphasized the continuity of Brazil's inflation-targeting and floating-exchange-rate regime, despite political transitions.

On June 3, 2008, Fitch Ratings followed Standard and Poor's lead, citing a similar rationale:

> The rating upgrade reflects the dramatic improvement in Brazil's external and public sector balance sheet that has greatly reduced Brazil's vulnerability to external and exchange rate shocks and entrenched macroeconomic stability and enhanced medium-term growth prospects. The authorities have established a track record of commitment to low inflation and a primary budget surplus that has dispelled previous concerns over medium-term fiscal sustainability. Brazil's investment-grade ratings are also supported by its diverse, high value added economy . . . and its relative political and social stability. A growing consensus across the political spectrum on macroeconomic policies also reduces the potential for a marked departure from the current setting.[22]

In short order, the two other leading credit-rating agencies, Moody's and Dominion Bond Rating Service, did so as well. Investors were delighted, seeing Brazil as a very attractive buying opportunity. But analysts were quick to point out that the government would have to work hard to sustain the country's economic performance in order to retain its hard-won investment-grade status. Despite its recent progress, numerous problems continued to plague Brazil, including high public debt, a rigid fiscal structure, uneven progress on reducing structural economic distortions such as further tax and pension reforms, social pressures for higher investment in

FIGURE 7-3. Proven Reserves of Crude Oil and Petroleum Production, 1989–2009

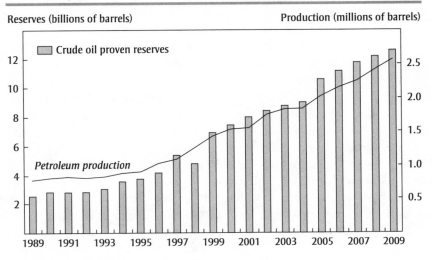

Source: U.S. Energy Information Administration, Brazil Energy Profile.

education, health, and security that constrain growth, an upward trend in government primary spending, relatively high government debt ratios, and generally the glacial pace of structural reforms. Thus a daunting agenda will confront the next president and his or her government.

Brazil's Energy Bonanza

An important development that may help to ease this task is Brazil's emergence as a potential world leader in energy production (see figure 7-3.) In 2007–08 Petrobras, the state oil company, announced the discovery of massive natural gas and petroleum reserves off the southeast coast. Giving the oil fields colorful names such as Tupi and Jupitor, the country suddenly became an energy player on a global scale. Brazil had already reached energy self-sufficiency in 2006, and the new discoveries held out the possibility that Brazil would become an important exporter of fossil fuels over the next decade. According to a recent estimate, the Tupi oil field, named for one of Brazil's indigenous populations, holds 5 billion to 8 billion barrels of recoverable oil and natural gas reserves.[23] This discovery could boost Brazil's 12.2 billion barrels of proven reserves by nearly two-thirds, putting Brazil ahead of Canada (17.1 billion barrels) and Mexico (12.9 billion barrels).[24] The discovery makes Brazil one of the five or six countries with the highest estimated petroleum reserves, falling between China and Nigeria on a world scale.

In addition, Brazil's three-decades-old ethanol program has come into its own in the past few years. The government provided three important initial drivers for the ethanol industry: guaranteed purchases by Petrobras, low-interest loans for ethanol firms, and a fixed-price schedule that set the price of hydrous ethanol at 59 percent of the price of gasoline at the pump. These policies have helped Brazil to become the world's second largest producer of ethanol and the world's largest exporter of the sugar-based fuel.[25] Together, Brazil and the United States produce 70 percent of the world's ethanol and nearly 90 percent of ethanol used for fuel.

Brazil is also considered to have the world's first sustainable biofuel economy. Its ethanol program uses the most efficient technology for sugarcane cultivation in the world. It employs modern equipment and cheap sugarcane as feedstock and uses the residual cane waste to process heat and power, which results in a very competitive price and also in a high balance of energy (output energy to input energy).[26] No new vehicles in Brazil run on pure gasoline. The Brazilian car industry developed flexible-fuel vehicles that run on any proportion of gasoline and hydrous ethanol. Introduced in the internal market in 2003, flex vehicles rapidly became a commercial success. In 2009 the fleet of flex cars and light commercial vehicles reached 7.1 million vehicles, representing about 21 percent of Brazil's registered light motor vehicle fleet. All car users have the option of using any combination of fuels on a daily basis.

In early 2007 the government announced plans to triple ethanol exports in the next seven years at a cost of $13 billion to $14 billion in new investment. The announcement reignited controversy over the impact of expanded sugar production on food production. However, the program's defenders maintained that the Brazilian frontier was immense, providing more than adequate room both for growing foodstuffs and for producing sugar for the ethanol industry.

These two developments—the ethanol industry and the impressive natural gas and oil discoveries of the last few years—have positioned Brazil to be a global energy player in the twenty-first century. Petrobras is recognized as one of the premier state-owned oil companies in the world. The car industry in Brazil has proven to be a model in producing flex vehicles. The vast agricultural frontier guarantees a permanent supply of sugar for the ethanol industry that will be part of a global solution to energy demand in the coming years. Twenty years ago there was little recognition of the energy potential of Brazil. Today it is a proven fact.

The Growth of Brazil's Financial Sector

Just as recent energy policies are shaping the ability of Brazil to fuel its economic growth, the growth and transformation of the financial sector are the keys to financing it. The development of the banking system and capital markets since the *Real* Plan of 1994–95 has played a key role in allocating scarce resources to productive and efficient Brazilian enterprises. Brazil's financial sector growth is closely linked to its economic development: the growth of the stock market and financial liberalization are directly correlated with the growth of GDP, investment rates, and private consumption. At the same time, the banking sector has been used as an instrument of government policy, which has contributed to the substantial growth of the manufacturing and industrial sectors.

During the hyperinflation of the early 1990s, it would have been hard to imagine that Brazilian banks and capital markets would be the world players they have become. In 2009 three of the world's top ten banks in terms of market capitalization were Brazilian.[27] Increasingly solid financial fundamentals allowed Brazil to bounce back quickly from the financial crisis of 2007–09. This strength positioned Brazil among the major world powers at the G-20, allowing it to play a role in negotiating future financial regulation following the global financial crisis. Today, Brazil's stock market is the largest in the region and the fourth largest in the world, and the banking sector is witnessing an increase in competition and expansion of private credit. While many limitations remain to the expansion of financial services to small and medium-size enterprises, important institutional reforms in the areas of regulation, bankruptcy law, and corporate governance have had a very positive impact on the sector's growth prospects.

As Brazil has become more politically and economically integrated with countries to its north and east, so too has it become more integrated with world financial markets. Brazilian companies have benefited from high growth, driven largely by domestic demand and high commodity prices, which has obliged them to look abroad for increased sources of capital. Foreign banks, the largest of which is the Spanish Banco Santander, play an increasingly expansive role in the banking sector. At the same time,

Brazil has turned into a hotbed for foreign investment since the beginning of the twenty-first century. Despite a significant capital flight at the end of 2008, investment numbers recuperated in the wake of the 2007–08 financial crisis. During October 2009 alone, Brazil received $2.44 billion in equity investments (nearly double those received by China). Brazil's accessibility to foreign investors distinguishes it from its BRIC peers. As one investor put it, "It may have slower growth than China, but it's a lot easier to invest in."[28]

The past twenty years have seen significant financial liberalization and a deepening of Brazil's banking sector. Prompted by a growing economy, expanding middle class, and increasingly prudent fiscal policies, the environment has been ripe for the growth of the Brazilian banks, both public and private. Aggressive bank reforms—first in 1988 and later in 1994–95—have proven to be a springboard for the expansion of Brazil's banking sector. Consequently, the size of the banking sector in terms of assets and clients has grown more than threefold since 2000.

Foreign banks were motivated to invest in Brazil following the 1990s reforms and the consequent improvement in macroeconomic stability. The entrance of new actors has increased the amount of competition in the sector, which has resulted in diminishing interest rates and returns for banks located in Brazil. The representation of foreign credit operations has increased from 7.1 percent of the banking system in 1988 to 19.2 percent in July of 2009.[29] Despite a recent setback in the wake of the financial crisis, Santander's initial public offering (IPO) in October 2009 was the largest of that year and the largest IPO ever for a Brazilian company, a deal that carried a value of $8 billion.[30] Unlike domestic private banks, which are able to fuel their operations primarily from individual deposits, private foreign banks fund their operations primarily from corporate deposits and overseas sources.

However, Brazil has not been immune to its own episodes of capital flight. Many banks left during the Argentine crisis of 2001. Morgan Stanley and Goldman Sachs have been accused of withdrawing capital in recent history, and UBS's decision to sell Pactual this year proves that Brazilian regulators may have reason to be cautious of entrance by foreign banks. While foreign banks have provided greater competition in the banking sector, private domestic banks continue to be the more powerful player in the market; of the five most sustainable banks in Latin America, four are Brazilian, of which two are private domestic banks and one is a state-owned bank.[31] However, foreign banks still face certain barriers to entry, such as a disadvantage in treasury operations, lack of access to privileged customers, and a "toll" for entry.

Capital markets in Brazil have experienced tremendous growth in nominal terms over the past two decades. Institutional improvements, financial sector liberalization, and macroeconomic stability have made Brazil a safe haven for domestic and foreign investors. The opening of Brazilian capital markets began as early as May 1991, considered the official date of "equity market liberalization."[32] That year, foreign investment laws were changed to allow foreign institutions to own up to 49 percent of voting and 100 percent of nonvoting stock in Brazilian corporations, and foreign institutional investors were given the ability to administer portfolios of Brazilian securities.[33] Foreign direct investment was also allowed, with no tax on capital gains and a 15 percent tax on distributed earnings. Less than a year later, the first American depository receipt (ADR) was introduced.[34] Since 1991 real investment has grown approximately 2.5 percent in Brazil, compared to nearly 2 percent in the years before liberalization.[35]

Given the limited capital available to the private sector through the banking system, the primary markets have become important sources of long-term financing for the largest private companies. The development of capital markets is often viewed as an important precondition for the growth of the Brazilian economy. In 2002 José Luís Osório, chairman of the Securities and Exchange Commission, made the following statement: "Today there are only two ways that a Brazilian can become a big businessman. He can be born rich, or he can gain access to the National Bank of Economic and Social Development (BNDES) financing. We want to create a third way—through capital markets."[36]

Brazilian capital markets have become increasingly linked to their international siblings via improved technology and the ability of Brazilian firms to list abroad. The Global Trading System links the Brazilian Securities, Commodities, and Futures Exchange (BM&FBovespa) with the Globex Alliance, which links international markets in Chicago, Madrid, Montreal, Paris, and Singapore, and allows Brazilian investors to invest directly in the member markets. Using products such as futures and options contracts on interest rates, commodities, equity indexes, and foreign exchange has increased the viability of these connections. Similarly, there has been a large increase in the listing of Brazilian companies abroad, generally through ADRs and global depository receipts.[37] As of February 2009, eighty-six Brazilian firms had ADRs, an increase from eighty-two in the previous year. The leader among these was Petro-bras, the state-owned oil company. As of March 2009, thirty-six Brazilian companies were listed on the New York Stock Exchange, making Brazil the largest Latin American issuer in the United States.[38]

While the financial sector has expanded greatly in the last few decades, Brazil has shown prudence in its growth and taken efforts to reduce the risk of major financial shocks, such as those experienced in the 1980s. As a result of its healthy growth, confidence has grown in Brazil's financial system. One sign of this confidence is Brazil's ability to sell debt in domestic currency. Brazil began to sell *real*-denominated sovereign debt in 2005; most recently it sold R$1.5 billion of debt with a seven-year maturity in October 2009. Such sales allow Brazil to hedge against a potential increase in international interest rates or a rapid appreciation of the dollar (or depreciation of the *real*).

There is, however, still room for growth in the Brazilian financial sector. Although the soundness of banks and financial market sophistication in Brazil are among its competitive advantages as a place to do business, access to financing continues to be one of the challenges that companies face. Structural issues such as corruption and weak contract laws continue to pervade Brazilian institutions and to challenge the solidity of the financial sector. Many small and medium enterprises still face limited access to financing. Additionally, in 2009 bank nonperforming loans rose to 4.3 percent of total loans, higher than in nearly every other Latin American country.[39]

The involvement of the state in banking has had mixed effects on the financial system. On the one hand, strict regulations and monitoring meant that banks were well prepared to face the latest financial crisis and remain well capitalized. Thanks to strict capital requirements, the central bank was not required to intervene in or to liquidate any Brazilian banks after March 2008. On the other hand, state-run banks continue to dominate long-term and development financing, where they enjoy certain advantages. One result of this policy may be pervasive high interest rates. Another potential side effect is the crowding out of private investment, especially in areas that need more competition (that is, financing of small and medium enterprises).

Much remains to be done to encourage the healthy growth of capital markets as well. Liquidity and market concentration are persistent problems; as of October 2009 only 387 companies were listed on the BM&FBovespa. At the same time, government securities continue to crowd out private bonds in the securities market. At a higher level, Brazilian institutions are still susceptible to corruption and a weak rule of law.

The recent 2 percent tax on capital inflows is one sign that Brazil's Securities and Exchange Commission continues to exercise caution in the face of what appears to be a rising stock market bubble and that Brazil no longer maintains the Washington consensus ideal of complete market liberalization and reliance on foreign capital. After all, many hurdles still face Brazil on its path to economic and financial growth. As former president Fernando Henrique Cardoso has pointed out, Brazil faces a shortage of infrastructure and suffers from poor quality of education, environmental challenges, and crime.[40]

Brazil as an Emerging-Market Leader

Backed by these policy achievements, under Lula, Brazil emerged as a regional and global diplomatic player, as the next chapter discusses in greater detail. Lula's predecessor, Fernando Henrique Cardoso, began this process by boosting the country's participation in both regional and international affairs. He hosted the first South American summit in Brasília in August 2000, and under Cardoso Brazil became a strong advocate of the Common Market of the South (Mercosur) and the Ibero-American summit meetings that annually bring together the Spanish- and Portuguese-speaking countries of the Americas and Europe. But the continued weakness of the Brazilian economy, a result of both global turbulence and Cardoso's inability to move beyond initial reforms, limited Brazil's role in world affairs during his presidency.

Lula's commitment to economic orthodoxy as president, combined with his government's decision to stick to the best of its predecessor's policies, such as inflation targeting, while pursuing structural reform, led to marked improvement in Brazil's economic performance. The government also benefited from a major upswing in demand for many of Brazil's natural resources and manufactured goods, which helped to strengthen the country's trade balance and current account. The recent energy finds, as well as Brazil's progress in ethanol production, have combined with these gains to elevate the country's status among the emerging-market countries.

Equally important, Brazil's impressive—some would say extraordinary—economic modernization has ended the great debate about the appropriate model for the country. Brazil has an increasingly diversified economy, with room to grow and deepen. Prudent and consistent fiscal and monetary policies have resulted in high levels of foreign direct investment and an investment-grade rating for its sovereign debt. At the same time, improvements in governance, despite perennial corruption scandals, have made it possible to address the long-standing issue of poverty reduction and begin the process of giving tens of millions of Brazilians the opportunity to benefit from a competitive economy and a consumer-led society. Looking forward at the end of the Lula years, Brazil appears poised to consolidate its lead role as an emerging-market economy.

8

Brazil's Emergence on the Global Stage

A s Brazil's economy gathered strength, the country's international profile began to rise. Under President Luiz Inácio da Silva (Lula), Brazil assumed an increasingly prominent role in both regional and global affairs. This chapter focuses on the most important initiatives in which Brazil has been involved since the start of the new century. These include a leadership role in discussing both a new global trade regime and the need for greater representation of Brazil, Russia, India, and China (the BRICs) in international financial decisionmaking. Brazil was prominent in the ultimately failed trade negotiations at the World Trade Organization (WTO)—known as the Doha Development Round. In order to revive the round, a strong consensus is needed between the BRIC countries and the developed states. After the financial crisis that began in 2008, the G-20 economies held a series of meetings to discuss needed reforms to the international financial system. Again, Brazil took a leadership role, joining its fellow BRIC countries in calling for a shift in voting power at the International Monetary Fund (IMF) in favor of the emerging economies. At the end of 2009 the media took note of Brazil's growing prominence among the developing economies.[1]

Brazil as a Regional Leader

Brazil has long been active in efforts to promote economic integration in South America. The active pursuit of this goal dates back to 1985, when

President Sarney and his Argentine counterpart Raúl Alfonsín signed a bilateral agreement on economic cooperation and integration. Six years later, this agreement was succeeded by the Treaty of Asunción, which created the Common Market of the South (Mercosur). The treaty's goal was to promote free trade among Mercosur's members—Brazil, Argentina, Paraguay, and Uruguay. The early years were upbeat, but the Brazilian devaluation in January 1999 and the collapse of the Argentine economy in 2001 dramatically slowed the integration process. In recent years, Mercosur has been unable to move beyond the original goals of deeper economic cooperation. It has been unable, for example, to establish dispute resolution mechanisms or deeper institutional decisionmaking processes. Most recently, it has become a highly political organization apparently more interested in discussing regional diplomatic and political controversies than trade. For many, Mercosur appeared to be at a dead end when it moved to admit Venezuela. Hugo Chávez, the country's controversial president, is less interested in trade and economic integration than in highly ideological statements aimed at the United States, liberal economics, and related topics. While the Brazilian Senate reluctantly approved Venezuela's membership, the Paraguayan Senate has yet to do so.

The Failure of the Free Trade Area of the Americas: Saying "No" to the United States

A similar goal drove efforts to create a Free Trade Area of the Americas (FTAA), which got under way at a summit of the Americas meeting in Miami in December 1994. However, after nine years of contentious negotiations, the FTAA proposal failed. The initial hope was to eliminate or reduce the barriers to trade among all countries in the Americas (with the exception of Cuba), building on the North American Free Trade Agreement between Canada, Mexico, and the United States, which came into effect in January 1994. However, sharp differences quickly emerged between the United States, which wanted to expand trade in services and protect intellectual property rights, and the Latin American governments, which sought to eliminate agricultural subsidies and liberalize trade in agricultural goods.

The tensions burst into the open at the Quebec City summit of the Americas held in 2001. Massive antimarket and antiglobalization protests made it clear that there was little support for free trade as defined by the United States. Efforts to resuscitate the FTAA at a Miami ministerial meeting in November 2003 and at the Mar del Plata summit of the Americas in November 2005 both failed. The United States then turned to a "hub and spoke" approach to trade liberalization, negotiating subregional treaties, including free trade agreements with Peru, Colombia, and Panama. The Bush administration achieved one successful subregional agreement with the approval of the Dominican Republic–Central American Free Trade Agreement (DR–CAFTA), which was signed into law by President George W. Bush on August 2, 2005. The other countries ratified the treaty over the next three years, and the agreement took effect on January 1, 2009. Meanwhile, many of the larger Latin American states turned to the Doha trade talks, which were taking place under the auspices of the WTO, with the hope of forging a broader alliance to pressure the industrial countries for concessions.

Regional political dynamics influenced the collapse of the FTAA negotiations as much as technical and policy differences. Brazil's 1999 financial crisis proved to be a major distraction for the Cardoso government until it limped out of office in 2003, limiting its ability to move the talks forward. The collapse of the Argentine economy in 2001 further dampened enthusiasm for any agreement that appeared to serve the interests of the United States. As skepticism of the so-called Washington consensus mounted, many Latin American policymakers soured on any United States–led initiative in general and on free trade in particular. This trend was presaged by the election of Hugo Chávez, a fierce critic of the United States, as Venezuela's president in 1998.[2] In Brazil it gained force with the impressive victory of Lula and the Workers Party (PT) in 2002. Despite its embrace of fiscal responsibility, the Lula administration showed little interest in the FTAA. In its place, it favored economic integration on a continental basis that excluded the United States.

Steps toward the United States of South America?

The idea of a unified South America has inspired visionaries since the days of Simón Bolívar, "the Liberator," in the early nineteenth century. The latest effort, with strong backing from Brazil, took form at the third South American summit in December 2004 (following the 2000 summit in Brasília and the 2002 summit in Guayaquil, Ecuador). The centerpiece of the summit, which was held over two days in Peru, was signature of the Cuzco Declaration, a two-page statement setting in motion the creation of the South American Community of Nations (SACN). SACN brought together two subregional trade blocs, Mercosur and the Andean

Community of Nations (comprising Bolivia, Colombia, Ecuador, and Peru), as well as Chile, Guyana, and Suriname. The Cuzco Declaration called for the new organization to develop a common currency, a tariff-free common market, and a regional parliament. According to the secretary general of the Andean Community at that time, the "ultimate goal, which can hopefully be reached, in time, is the United States of South America."[3]

At their first summit, held in Brasília in September 2005, the SACN heads of state agreed on steps to formalize their agreement. Accordingly, twelve nations signed the constitutive treaty of the Union of South American Nations (UNASUR), which replaced SACN, at the third summit of heads of state, also hosted by President Lula, on May 23, 2008. The hope of the members is that UNASUR will evolve, over time, into a South American European Union (EU). The treaty set goals for the integration of regional energy and transportation networks, immigration policies, and related matters. The goal is to establish a UNASUR parliament in Cochabamba, Bolivia, in time. Modeled on the EU, the executive will rotate every six months among the membership. UNASUR's structure is relatively simple: the heads of state meet annually, and the foreign ministers meet every six months for planning and consultation. In addition, at a meeting called by President Lula in Salvador, Brazil, in December 2008, the heads of state adopted the Brazilian proposal to form a South American Defense Council with the goal of consolidating "South America as a zone of peace, a base for democratic stability and comprehensive development of the peoples, as a contribution to world peace."

The council, which met for the first time in Santiago, Chile, in March 2009, will adopt a standardized method to measure the arms purchases of each country, coordinate the activities of their militaries on peace and humanitarian missions, and strengthen the regional capacity to produce defense systems and military technology, in part by promoting bilateral and multilateral investment in the region's defense industries. There are also plans to link military training academies in the region and to establish a South American Center of Strategic Studies.

Brazil's leadership role in the UNASUR initiative has been critical. As the acknowledged leader in South American regional efforts (reluctantly accepted by President Hugo Chávez of Venezuela who has, in the past, hoped that his country would play that role), the government of President Lula has taken a broad historical vision of the goal of deeper regional integration.

There is no guarantee that the UNASUR process will prosper. Indeed, at a summit of the Latin American and Caribbean heads of state in Cancún, Mexico, in February 2010, unanimous support was given to the creation of a new organization, the Community of Latin American and Caribbean States. The relationship between the Cancún initiative and UNASUR is not yet clear, but the Brazilian role, again, will be critical to working out an appropriate linkage. There have numerous regional and subregional programs over the years. Many have failed. An important difference today is the strong role that Brazil plays in the new undertakings—a reality that did not exist before the emergence of the new Brazil. While the prospects for UNASUR are uncertain, the initiative reflects the new realities in the region where the desire for autonomous institution building is and will remain very strong. These initiatives should not be viewed as anti–United States, but rather as a process that is pro–Latin America and the Caribbean in the changing twenty-first century.

Broader Efforts at Regional Cooperation

At the same time, Brazil has continued to pursue broader regional initiatives. A recent example was the first Latin American and Caribbean Summit for Integration and Development (CALC), which brought the leaders of thirty-three Latin American and Caribbean states, including Raúl Castro of Cuba, to the Brazilian resort of Costa do Sauípe, Bahia, in December 2008. Symbolically, the United States, Canada, and the European Union were not invited to attend. The regional meeting was preceded by a string of mini-summits involving Mercosur, UNASUR, and the Rio Group, and plans were announced to integrate the CALC and the Rio Group in a new permanent regional body.

Created at a December 1986 meeting in Rio de Janeiro, the Rio Group grew out of regional efforts to negotiate an end to the Central American conflicts of the early 1980s and unilateral U.S. intervention in the region. The original signatories were the members of the so-called Contadora Group (Colombia, Mexico, Panama, and Venezuela) and the Contadora Support Group (Argentina, Brazil, Peru, and Uruguay). The United States was not invited to join the Rio Group, which many saw as an alternative to the Washington-based Organization of American States. However, Cuba was admitted as a member in November 2008. The Rio Group has no permanent secretariat or headquarters; instead, the heads of state of its twenty-three members meet once a year to discuss issues of mutual concern to the group in regional and international venues.[4]

Common Themes

Brazil's growing involvement in these major regional integration efforts stands in sharp contrast to the country's reluctance just twenty years ago to become more deeply involved in initiatives that extended beyond the Southern Cone. In part, this trend reflects disappointment with Mercosur, which has been weakened by internal economic crises, persistent disputes over issues such as double taxation of third-country imports within the bloc, and the unresolved question of whether Venezuela should be admitted as a member.[5] Brazil's hope is that UNASUR and CALC will eventually energize efforts at South American integration and cooperation and probably replace Mercosur.[6]

These initiatives share some important features. First, the United States, Canada, and the European Union were deliberately excluded from all of them. Second, these are principally South American, not Latin American, initiatives. For some years, Brasília has insisted on the differentiation between South America and North America. (This was the raison d'être of the first summit convened by President Cardoso in Brasília in 2000.) Mexico, Central America, and the Caribbean, for planning purposes, are viewed by many on the continent as part of North America and dominated by the United States. The CALC may represent a turning point in Brazil's vision for the future integration of the hemisphere, but that remains to be seen. Third, all of the South American initiatives have seen the exercise of strong leadership by President Lula and Itamarty, Brazil's well-regarded Ministry of Foreign Affairs. During Lula's presidency, other South American leaders have come to recognize Brazil as the continent's leading representative at the international level.

Hurdles to Overcome

Considerable skepticism remains concerning efforts to build stronger South American ties. Very different regimes are in place across the continent. Some countries, such as Ecuador, Bolivia, Nicaragua, and Venezuela, have neopopulist antimarket governments, while leaders in other countries, including Brazil, Colombia, Chile, and Peru, are strongly market oriented. Old rivalries persist. Issues such as the guerrilla war still under way in Colombia divide the region.

Moreover, some of Brazil's small neighbors have not hesitated to challenge the local "big brother." In 2006 Bolivia's Evo Morales nationalized the operations of Brazil's energy giant Petrobras along with other foreign oil holdings. In September 2008 Ecuador's president Rafael Correa expelled managers of the Brazilian engineering company Odebrecht over allegedly substandard power plant construction and refused to repay some of the loans extended by Brazil's national development bank. That same year, Paraguay's Fernando Lugo made calls for renegotiating the Itaipu energy supply treaty with Brazil a main plank of his successful presidential campaign.

Lula has skillfully managed such disputes. While embracing a pragmatic center-left stance like his counterparts in Chile and Uruguay, Lula has maintained good relations with the more populist leaders of Venezuela, Bolivia, and Ecuador—as several mini-summits of these four nations and Brazil's invitation to Venezuela to join Mercosur both attest. Brazil has also helped more literally to maintain the peace in South America. In spring 2008, when the opposition in Bolivia threatened to destabilize the government, Brazil left no doubt about its support for President Evo Morales, even alluding to the possibility of using military force to maintain constitutional order. Finally, by successfully running the United Nations Stabilization Mission in Haiti (MINUSTAH), Brazil has shown that it is ready to use military forces to promote peace in the hemisphere.[7] At the same time, Brazil has been careful not to voice ambitions to continental leadership. A more modest approach, the government hopes, will facilitate regional integration and maintain the perception that Brazil seeks to act simply as a neighbor among equals.

Brazil and the Other BRICs

As part of its broader effort to boost its presence on the world stage, Brazil has reached beyond South America to strengthen ties with the other BRICs, as well as with other members of the developing world. A leading example is IBSA, a dialogue forum between India, Brazil, and South Africa. IBSA was created in Brasília, under President Lula's leadership, in 2003 with the Declaration of Brasília. According to a Spanish observer,

> Although IBSA is not yet recognized as a major international actor, this high-level forum reflects the fact that Brazil, India, and South Africa have begun to assume a pro-active and increasingly collective bargaining role, in an international context. Thus Brazil, India, and South Africa's common stance on regional and international conflicts provides evidence of the beginnings of southern approaches to global problems.[8]

The annual IBSA summit meetings have emphasized stronger trade relations, support for democracy and human rights, peace, and development. A high priority has been the development of a dialogue between IBSA and the European Union. The goal in such relationships is for India, Brazil, and South Africa to act as a counterweight to the industrial countries by using soft balancing power, instead of trying to act as a rival hegemon.[9] Following the nuclear summit organized by President Barack Obama in April 2010 in Washington, a fourth summit meeting was held in Brasília on April 13–14. Among the topics discussed was an expansion of the IBSA Facility for Poverty and Hunger Alleviation. Climate change and trade negotiations were also on the agenda.

Russia has also emerged on the Brazilian radar and vice versa. Russia's president, Dmitry Medvedev, visited Brazil following the Asia-Pacific Economic Cooperation summit in fall 2008 in Lima, Peru. While in Rio de Janeiro, Medvedev said that he hoped that trade between the two countries would double from a modest baseline of $5 billion in 2007. He also announced plans to coordinate the two countries' efforts "in fighting the crisis and creating a new global financial architecture."[10] On the same trip, Medvedev went to Venezuela to sign arms, energy, and mining deals. But as one analyst points out, by inviting Medvedev, Lula clearly told Moscow, "If you want to have a significant relationship in South America, have it with us."[11]

Even more important than the emerging ties with Russia is Brazil's relationship with China. China and Brazil have been strategic partners since the mid-1990s, and since Jiang Zemin's trip to Brazil in 2001, leaders of both countries have met regularly. Most recently, China's Vice President Xi Jinping came to Brazil in early 2009, and Lula visited his counterpart Hu Jintao in Beijing in May. Despite the gloom cast by the global economic crisis, Brazilian exports to China have grown rapidly. In spring 2009 China became Brazil's biggest trading partner for the first time, displacing the United States. Chinese investment, which has so far lagged behind Latin American hopes, is expected to increase, and Brazil's newly discovered oil fields offer significant potential for further cooperation. As a first step, an agreement was reached in May 2009 for Brazil to supply 100,000 to 160,000 barrels of oil a day at market prices, in exchange for a $10 billion loan from the China Development Bank to help to develop its major oil reserves.[12] The two countries have even started to consider abandoning the dollar for bilateral trade and using yuan and reais instead—the latest sign that China and Brazil are increasingly ready to challenge the status quo in world affairs.[13] Following the nuclear summit that took place in Washington in April 2010, President Hu Jintao traveled to Brazil for a state visit and to participate in the second summit of the BRIC countries. He also held meetings with the governments of Chile and Venezuela, but the stop in Brasília was viewed as the priority of his trip to the region.

Beyond these bilateral projects, the four BRICs have joined together as a group to amplify their voice. After meeting twice on the sidelines of the United Nations General Assembly in New York, the four countries' foreign ministers had their first stand-alone meeting at Yekaterinburg, Russia, in May 2008. A joint communiqué adopted at the meeting states, "Building a more democratic international system founded on the rule of law and multilateral diplomacy is an imperative of our time." The Brazilian foreign minister, Celso Amorim, commented at the end of the meeting, "We are changing the way the world order is organized."

New initiatives now appear more frequently. In March 2010 the four BRICs announced that they will pool resources to combat famine. At a meeting in Moscow that month, agricultural ministers signed a pact to create a joint agricultural information base that will help each country to calculate production and consumption balances and establish natural grain reserves. The four ministers agreed to share experience in providing food to vulnerable populations and victims of natural disasters as well as exchanging agricultural technology to reduce the effect of climate change on food production. The BRIC economies produce 40 percent of the world's wheat, half of its pork, and one-third of its poultry and beef.[14]

At a second BRIC summit held in Brazil in April 2010, the BRIC countries discussed the feasibility of broadening the array of world currencies used in international trade in the future. This is another indication of the interest and capacity of the four emerging-market economies to explore new policy options that are not defined by the industrial states.

Brazil at the Center of North-South Relations

This ambition has been particularly evident in the areas of trade and finance.[15] In these two arenas, once dominated by the United States and Europe, emerging-market countries, led by the BRICs, have been increasingly demanding a larger role in international decisionmaking. The collapse of the Doha trade round, which was undertaken under the auspices of the WTO, is one indication of the growing power these countries wield;

the recent resuscitation of the G-20 in the wake of the 2008–09 financial crisis is another.

The DOHA Development Round

The Doha Development Round began at a ministerial meeting in Doha, Qatar, in November 2001, after violent protests by antiglobalization and antitrade groups doomed an earlier effort to launch a new round of trade negotiations in Seattle. The Doha development agenda committed all countries to a new round of negotiations on opening agricultural and manufacturing markets as well as trade in services (General Agreement on Trade in Services) and expanded intellectual property regulation (Agreement on Trade-related Aspects of Intellectual Property Rights). According to proponents, the intent of the round, which was scheduled to end in January 2005, was to make trade rules fairer for developing countries. Opponents argued that the round would worsen trade terms for the developing world and, once again, favor the interests of the industrial states.

The ministers gathered again in Cancún, Mexico, in September 2003 to draft a concrete agreement on the Doha round objectives. But the session collapsed after four days without agreement on a common framework for continuing negotiations. Serious differences on the "Singapore issues"—transparency in government procurement, trade facilitation (customs issues), trade and investment, and trade and competition—which had been inherited from a previous round of talks, seemed irresolvable.[16] Making matters worse, the good faith of some participants was questioned, with critics charging that they had come to Cancún not to negotiate but to repeat old demands. But most important, a wide gap remained between developing and developed countries on virtually all topics, such as the perennially thorny issue of agricultural trade.

Following the breakdown at Cancún, talks resumed in March 2004. In July 2004 a meeting was held in Geneva; led by Brazil and India, the parties agreed to a framework agreement. The two BRICS negotiated directly with the developed countries on agriculture and attempted to find common ground on the controversial issue of agricultural subsidies in the EU and the United States. The initiative failed, and the Singapore issues were removed from the Doha agenda. The European Union appeared to accept the elimination of agricultural export subsidies "by date certain." The deadline for a final agreement was moved from January to December 2005.

The deadline came and went as the talks moved to Hong Kong in late 2005, back to Geneva in July 2006, and on to Potsdam in June 2007. In Potsdam, the United States, the European Union, Brazil, and India arrived at an impasse over farm subsidies, among other issues, and the negotiations once again broke down. The talks moved back to Geneva in July 2008, and some compromises emerged. The United States offered to cap its farm subsidies at $15 billion a year, down from $18.2 billion in 2006. But the United States expected the BRICs to show flexibility in other areas. Instead, new disagreements emerged over special protection for Chinese and Indian farmers and African and Caribbean banana imports to the European Union. In late July the talks collapsed. India and the United States deadlocked over the special safeguard mechanism, a measure designed to protect poor farmers by allowing countries to impose special tariffs on certain agricultural goods in the event of a surge in imports or a fall in prices. Seeking compromise, Brazil supported a proposal by Pascal Lamy, director general of the WTO, that would cap U.S. farm subsides at $14.5 billion in return for cuts in industrial tariffs in developing countries, but the effort failed.[17]

Reports from Geneva after the failure of the talks highlighted the emergence of important new players at the global level as well as the issues at stake:

> A seven-year effort to forge a new global trade pact collapsed over farm tariffs Tuesday, reflecting a dramatic shift in the influence and the interests of trading powerhouses China, India, and Brazil. . . . Trade diplomats across the board said Tuesday's failure showcased as rarely before the emergence of China, India, and Brazil as trade powerhouses.[18]

Following the conclusion of the Geneva meeting, the Brazilian delegation joined Pascal Lamy in urging that the talks resume. A declaration at the end of the April 2009 Financial G-20 meeting in London also called for a renewal of talks, but there appears to be little optimism about a new round of conversations in the foreseeable future.

As the world's second biggest exporter of soy and the leading exporter of beef, chicken, sugar, and coffee, Brazil was a key player throughout the Doha round. For Brazil the rise of other regional economic powerhouses, such as China and India, has meant new outlets for its goods, diluting the leverage of the United States and the European Union. Soaring commodity prices through 2008 also encouraged Brazil and other developing nations to press harder for concessions on key issues such as agricultural subsidies. At the same time, by supporting Lamy's compromise in Geneva, Brazil won praise for its leadership role and consolidated its reputation as a tough but pragmatic negotiator.

China and India, in contrast, were blamed for their inability to think globally and ultimately for the failure of the talks. The Indian trade minister, Kamal Nath, who emerged as the chief spokesman for the poorest and smallest nations, argued that poorer countries need to keep the right to use tariffs to protect nascent industries, like India's fledgling car sector. The Indian government also criticized rich nations for coddling their farmers at a time of record food prices. (Domestic politics were a factor in this stance: the government was facing a difficult election in 2009, and small farmers were a key constituency for the ruling coalition led by the Congress Party.) These arguments applied with much less force to China, which as the world's second largest exporter after Germany shared many trade interests with the United States and the EU. But China sided with India to show solidarity, for geopolitical reasons, with the developing world.[19] In addition, as its trade with other emerging-market countries—from Asian neighbors like Indonesia and Malaysia to the Persian Gulf and Africa—has boomed in recent years, China appears to be looking for future growth outside the United States and Europe, which gives the government less incentive to work with the industrial countries that still dominate the WTO process.

Pushing a Bigger Role for the G-20

In the financial arena, the G-20 has gained an increasingly important role in the last few years. It was created as a response to the financial crises of the late 1990s and in recognition of the fact that key emerging-market countries were largely excluded from global economic governance.[20] Since its creation in 1999, its main purpose has been to bring together important industrial and developing economies to discuss key issues in the global economy. Brazil quickly emerged as a spokesman for the group, which fluctuates in size but has retained the original title. Brazil has pushed for the G-20 to replace the G-7, which is limited to industrial nations, as the leading forum for discussing and solving global issues such as the economic crisis.[21] In addition, Brazilian policymakers maintain that the answers to the world's most pressing issues can only be found if emerging economies such as Brazil and India are given more influence within multilateral financial institutions such as the IMF and the World Bank. As

Brazil's Foreign Minister Celso Amorim, argues, "If you want to have Brazil, India, China, South Africa participating in the effort they have to have more voice also in these financial institutions."[22]

This debate became particularly pressing after the outbreak of the global financial crisis, beginning in the United States, in 2008. French President Nicolas Sarkozy, then serving as president of the European Union, called for a "rethink" of the financial system in September. A month later, Prime Minister Gordon Brown of Great Britain argued that the world needed a new Bretton Woods system; the challenge, he said, was to build a new international financial architecture. There was general agreement that the G-20 should be convened, and after some diplomatic sparring over the venue, the White House announced that the United States would host the meeting in Washington on November 14–15, 2008.

Brazil convened a meeting of the G-20 finance ministers in São Paulo a few days before the Washington summit. The meeting laid out a set of agreed principles, including the need for more financial market regulation and coordinated government action and the importance of giving smaller, emerging-market economies more voice in how to resolve the crisis. Within the context of the São Paulo conclave, the four BRIC finance ministers forged a joint position that called for reform of institutions like the IMF to reflect the growing importance of developing economies. "Emerging countries are ready to shoulder the financial consequences of a bigger participation at the IMF," Brazilian Finance Minister Guido Mantega told a news conference, "There is no point in us increasing our participation if the big countries keep their veto powers."[23] The BRIC finance ministers "called for the reform of multilateral institutions in order that they reflect the structural changes in the world economy and the increasingly central role that emerging markets now play."[24] In addition, they called for an expansion of the Financial Stability Forum to include the big emerging economies along with the G-7 industrial nations and a handful of other major economies.[25]

Subsequently, after lively debate, the G-20 summit in Washington produced a declaration by the gathered leaders: "We are determined to enhance our cooperation and work together to restore global growth and achieve needed reforms in the world's financial systems."[26] Preparations were then made for a follow-up summit in London in April 2009. Following the Washington summit, the four BRIC countries participated in a summit in Moscow called the "BRIC Countries on the World Political Map: New Challenges." On the agenda were items such as the following:

Are the BRICs an alternative to a unipolar world? What are the mechanisms for consultation and dialogue among the BRIC countries, and what is their organizational format? And what is the economic basis and outlook for BRIC countries in light of the crises in the world financial-economic system?

At a planning meeting of G-20 international financial officials in Horsham, England, in March 2009, the BRIC countries called on the United States and Europe to improve information sharing and demanded a bigger role in guiding the International Monetary Fund. In a joint statement, the four countries also called for significantly more resources for the IMF and said that they wanted more voting weight, stating, "We call for urgent action with regard to voice and representation in the IMF in order that they better reflect their real economic weights."[27] The BRIC representatives also stressed that the next leaders of the IMF and the World Bank should be chosen "through open merit-based processes, irrespective of nationality or regional considerations."[28] Traditionally, Europe has appointed the head of the IMF, and the United States has chosen the World Bank chief. The United States has indicated its willingness to support a non-American candidate for the World Bank when the current U.S. president's term ends. The EU has yet to make a firm commitment to do the same at the IMF.

The London summit issued the Global Plan for Recovery and Reform.[29] The principal achievement was a commitment to provide $1.1 trillion to various programs to improve international finance, credit, trade, and overall economic stability and recovery. Further meetings are planned to assess the implementation of the policy directives of the summit.

A third G-20 summit was held in Pittsburgh, Pennsylvania, in September 2009, chaired by President Barack Obama. The final communiqué stated that the leaders had agreed to launch a framework that would identify policies that will generate strong, sustainable, and balanced global growth. A key component of the framework will be to strengthen the international financial regulatory system. Reflecting the position of the BRIC countries, the summit participants agreed to reform the mandate, mission, and governance structure of the IMF as well as the multilateral development banks. To review the progress on the framework, the G-20 scheduled summits in Canada in June 2010 and in Korea in November 2010 with the expectation that the group will meet annually thereafter.

While Brazil's active involvement in the G-20 and the response to the financial crisis has been one noticeable aspect of its strengthening role, a change in rhetoric underlines the country's new self-esteem. Since its very beginning, Lula accused the wealthy nations of being responsible for the global financial crisis. He pointed out "that those responsible" for the global financial crisis had to take swift action to end the economic free-fall. "It's not fair for Latin American, African, and Asian countries to pay for the irresponsibility of sectors of the American financial system," he said.[30] Over the months, his tone got even harsher, in particular when meeting with U.K. Prime Minister Gordon Brown in preparation of the G-20 summit, when he provocatively said, "This crisis was caused by no black man or woman or by no indigenous person or by no poor person. . . . This crisis was fostered and boosted by irrational behaviour of some people that are white, blue-eyed. Before the crisis they looked like they knew everything about economics, and they have demonstrated they know nothing about economics."[31] Lula strongly defends a greater role for the emerging-market countries in international decisionmaking.

Brazil, the European Union, and the United States

Despite the controversy provoked by some of Lula's commentary on the financial crisis, ties between Brazil and the industrial states have continued to improve. This is particularly true when it comes to the relationship between Brasília and Brussels. Mercosur has provided the primary framework for ties between Brazil and the European Union since the 1990s. But more recently, EU policymakers have come to regard Brazil as their principal interlocutor in South America. Brazil is seen as an increasingly important partner for Europe in dealing with all of the major policy challenges that will need to be addressed in the twenty-first century.

In 1995 the European Union and Mercosur signed an interregional framework cooperation agreement, which entered into force in 1999. In 2000 the parties opened negotiations for an association agreement based on three areas of interest: political dialogue, cooperation, and a free trade area. While negotiations on the political and cooperation chapters are virtually concluded, the trade chapter remains unfinished, with the major sticking point being European agricultural subsidies. The European Union also provides assistance to Mercosur through its 2007–13 Regional Program. This program provides substantial financial support for projects in three priority areas: strengthening institutions, preparing for implementation of the association agreement, and fostering the participation of civil society in the Mercosur integration process. The European Union is by far the largest supplier of development assistance to Mercosur.

Nonetheless, over the last few years the European Commission has clearly recognized the increased importance of Brazil as a power in its own right. A decision was taken in Brussels to establish a strategic partnership with Brazil, which implies an established high level of consultation on policy issues of relevance to both. The commission was careful not to imply that the new link with Brazil would replace its relationship with Mercosur, but a shift in priorities had clearly taken place. The new partnership was launched at a Brazil-EU summit in Lisbon in July 2007. On that occasion, the president of the European Commission, José Manuel Durão Barroso, emphasized the benefits to both sides:

> This first Summit is a historic step in our relations with Brazil. The strategic partnership is about facing each other as global partners and to raise the level of our co-operation in a host of areas of common interests. By increasing our joint efforts with Brazil, we can make a difference in global debates on poverty or climate change.[32]

Immediately following the summit, President Lula paid his first visit to the commission in Brussels.

Nearly a year and a half later, a second summit was held in Rio de Janeiro. The EU was represented by European Commission President Barroso and by French President Sarkozy. The principal outcome was a joint action plan setting out the goals of the EU-Brazil strategic partnership: to promote peace and comprehensive security through multilateralism; to seek ways to cooperate on social development goals and environmental issues; to promote sustainable development; to promote regional cooperation; to promote science, technology, and innovation; and to promote people-to-people and cultural exchanges. In addition, the French president threw his weight behind Brazil's claims to an enhanced international role: No one could imagine resolving problems today "without involving China, India, and, of course, Brazil," he said, adding, "I think we need Brazil as a permanent member of the Security Council."[33] The third EU–Brazil summit took place in Stockholm, Sweden, on October 6, 2009. The key issues on the agenda were climate change and the global financial economic crisis. It was announced that Brazil will host a United Nations high-level event on sustainable development in Rio de

Janeiro in 2012, and both the EU and Brazil agreed that the "green economy" should be a primary focus.

In contrast to the EU, the U.S. government has talked from time to time about the possibility of stronger linkages with Brazil but has done little, if anything, to develop a concrete plan of action. Visits between President George W. Bush and President Lula were frequent, and despite persistent trade disputes, the United States invited Brazil to develop a strategic political dialogue as early as 2005.[34] Nevertheless, relations between Brazil and the United States remained relatively distant, which some critics saw as a reflection of an implicit anti-Americanism in the Brazilian government's diplomacy. One reason for this distance may have been Lula's sympathy for some of Latin America's left-wing regimes, in particular that of Cuba, which helped Lula and the PT when they were struggling against a military regime.[35]

With a new U.S. president in office in 2009, most observers expected a new impetus for bilateral relations. But Brazil seems determined to define this relationship on its own terms. "I'm going to ask the United States to take a different view of Latin America," Lula said in March 2009 before meeting with President Barack Obama. "We're a democratic, peaceful continent, and the United States has to look at the region in a productive, developmental way, and not just think about drug trafficking or organized crime."[36]

Brazil: The Crafty Superpower?

A recent report describes Brazil as "the crafty superpower," arguing that Brazil is becoming a unique regional powerhouse and that "with no manual for becoming a global power, Lula's Brazil seems to be writing one of its own."[37] As Lula commented late last year in a visit to Europe, "Not long ago I used to dream of accumulating $100 billion in foreign reserves. Soon we will have $300 billion."[38] There is no doubt that Lula has been a "lucky" president, but it is even more true that his eight-year administration has continued the good policies initiated by his predecessor, Fernando Henrique Cardoso. Brazil has never seen sixteen years of policy continuity in the last century. Building on the *Real* Plan of 1993–94, the federal government has reined in spending, diversified the economy, adapted a pragmatic foreign policy, and found an array of new economic and political partners. During the two administrations, Brazil has emerged

as an important energy broker—petroleum, natural gas, and ethanol—
and the home of very competitive multinational corporations that now
operate around the globe.

Underlying the new optimism regarding Brazil's international prominence is the fact that the middle class in Brazil is now a reality; it appears
to be permanent. A recent report captured that sentiment when it titled
its report "A better today—Brazil's growing middle class want the good
life. Right now."[39] The story confirms a critical victory for Brazil under
Lula: the Gini index that measures a country's income inequality proves
that millions have moved out of poverty into an emerging middle sector
in Brazilian society. This means that there are and will be more and more
consumers in the Brazilian marketplace. This will be good for local business,
and it will be a magnet for international investors. In a country of 190 million people an expanding and spending social sector cannot be ignored.

A great deal remains to be done. The tax system needs to be restruc-
tured. The labor market needs greater flexibility to allow companies to
hire and fire more easily. Credit needs to be extended to the new middle
class. The public sector, in order to remain competitive, will have to give
priority to higher spending in education, especially in math and science.
Physical infrastructure is in a woeful state of disrepair. To allow companies, domestic and foreign, to export abroad, roads, ports, and other facilities need to be modernized or built from scratch. There is hope that the
upcoming soccer finals in 2014 and the Olympics in 2016 will spur the
government that takes office in January 2011 to give building and construction very high priority. All of these challenges are manageable if the
political will can be found in Brasília to put the country first and not the
personal interests of the politicians. Lula demonstrated in his first term of
office that reform is possible. He gained critical support for reducing
poverty through the highly effective and popular Bolsa Família cash transfer program. Change is possible in Brazil, and it now appears to be
inevitable. The reform agenda will not always move smoothly. Priorities
will be hotly debated. But the sense in Brazil is that the country has turned
a corner. As President Lula commented last year, Brazil is not just the
country of the present, "it is really living a magical moment."[40]

A Final Caveat

Perhaps not all stories have a completely happy ending. In late 2009 Brazil
took a series of somewhat baffling policy decisions that raised the ques-

tion of whether or not the country was truly prepared for a global role, other than in trade and energy. The first was the somewhat confusing role of Brazil, and many of its neighbors, in the events in Honduras. President Manuel Zelaya was expelled from Honduras on the morning of June 28, 2009. The issue was his effort to hold a referendum on whether or not to reform the constitution to allow the president to run for a second term, which was prohibited by the existing constitution. The forces behind his expulsion argued that he was moving in the direction of President Hugo Chávez of Venezuela, a personalist, populist regime with little respect for constitutional formalities. Zelaya supporters said that the president was trying to move the country forward with a new program of modernization and reform. Ultimately, the Honduran Supreme Court upheld a lower court injunction against the June 28 poll and issued a secret order for Zelaya's detention on June 26, when he ignored the injunction.

Later on the day of the expulsion, Congress convened and voted to remove Zelaya. Roberto Micheletti, the speaker of Congress and next in the presidential line of succession, was sworn in as interim president. On July 1 the interim government declared a "state of exception" suspending all civil liberties. Since the president was escorted to the airport in Tegucigalpa by a military escort, the immediate press and media coverage claimed the action was a classic coup d'état, so long prevalent in the region. The Organization of American States, the United Nations, the United States, and the European Union condemned the removal of Zelaya as a military coup. The Organization of American States suspended Honduras on July 4, 2009, after the caretaker government refused to reinstate Zelaya. Public opinion remained divided in Honduras, with demonstrations and protests for and against the ousted president.

Zelaya organized a vigorous diplomatic counteroffensive, meeting with high government officials in several countries. Costa Rican President Óscar Arias attempted to negotiate a diplomatic solution with no success. The interim government remained firm in its opposition to any compromise. With the support of the Chávez government, Zelaya secretly returned to Honduras on September 21, 2009, and took refuge in the Brazilian embassy. The following day the interim administration suspended five constitutional rights for forty-five days.

With national elections scheduled for November 29, 2009, the debate appeared to hinge on whether or not the Micheletti administration would allow Zelaya to return, symbolically, to Honduras. The United States attempted to negotiate a compromise in November, but that effort collapsed given the intransigence on both sides. Many, but not all, of the governments in the hemisphere announced that they would not recognize the electoral results as legitimate if Zelaya were not reinstated first. Brazil was a leading advocate of this position. Many wondered why the Lula government did not attempt to use its regional leadership to broker a peaceful deal. Indeed, the rhetoric emanating from Brasília became increasingly strident as the crisis continued. It was further complicated, of course, by the fact that Zelaya was housed in the Brazilian embassy; no one saw an easy exit strategy before the inauguration in early 2010. Following the successful election, in which Porfirio Lobo Sosa of the National Party won with 55.9 percent of the vote, some countries—Panama, Costa Rica, Peru, Colombia, and finally the United States—stated that they would recognize the outcome as legitimate. These countries urged their hemispheric neighbors to view the election outcome as a means to move forward after the apparently honest balloting. UNASUR, led by Brazil and Argentina, refused. Mexico supported the Brazilian position.

While the intricacies of the transition will fall into place eventually, the critical question is why Brazil chose to ally itself with the radical nationalist governments in the region and did not seek to serve as a mediator. Some would argue that the PT was looking forward to the national elections in Brazil in October 2010. Others said that the PT, in its final year in office, wanted to demonstrate its traditional populist roots. Some commentators noted that Brazil and other countries had suffered repressive military regimes in the not-too-distant past and that any hint of military involvement raised issues about the role of the armed forces in politics. The Honduras impasse and the role of Brazil raised some questions regarding Brazil's role as a regional leader, but in November 2009 an incident opened a discussion as to whether or not the country was prepared to assume a greater geopolitical, global role.

On November 23, 2009, Iranian President Mahmud Ahmadinejad arrived in Brasília to open a three-country visit to South America. Following Brazil, he visited Bolivia and Venezuela. Following a meeting between the two heads of state, Lula affirmed Brazil's support for Iran's right to a civilian nuclear program and criticized attempts to isolate Iran over its nuclear ambitions. He also encouraged the Iranian leader to engage with the West. Lula said he opposed sanctions that had been threatened by the industrial countries and the United Nations and supported diplomacy.

The Brazilian president justified the visit of his Iranian counterpart as a long-range Brazilian strategy to become engaged in Middle East peacekeeping. Brasília noted that the president of Israel, Shimon Peres, and the head of the Palestinian Authority, Mahmud Abbas, had recently visited Brazil. President Lula announced that he would visit the region in 2010 to become further engaged in negotiations. The two leaders signed a series of bilateral accords on energy, agriculture, and science and technology. The Brazilian president noted that Iran had become one of Brazil's biggest trading partners in the Middle East, with trade doubling between 2003 and 2007 to nearly $2 billion, composed mostly of food sales to Teheran.

The decision to receive the Iranian head of state triggered an immediate outcry. Protests erupted in Brazil as well as abroad. Members of the United Nations were highly critical, as were former Brazilian diplomats, who believed the Brazilian position would legitimize the Iranian government at a time when the U.S. and European powers were seeking to pressure Iran to limit its development of nuclear technology for civilian use. Human rights groups denounced the visit given the Iranian president's repeated denial of the Holocaust and virulent attacks against the state of Israel. As part of the drama attached to the visit, President Obama sent a letter to President Lula the day before the Iranian visit; President Lula responded a few days later. U.S. Secretary of State Hillary Clinton and Foreign Minister Celso Amorim also spoke by telephone that week. Clearly the United States was focused on the nuclear issue; President Lula expanded the agenda in his letter to include the need to liberalize trade further, find a solution to the Honduran quandary, cooperate at the December 2009 conference on climate change in Copenhagen, Denmark, and explore opportunities for collaboration in building institutions in Haiti.

The Brazilian government reacted defensively to the visit. The official position was that Brazil needed to engage all countries, not isolate some. Brasília pointed to the growing commercial ties between the two countries and to the long-standing historical relationship over decades. The Brazilian government also welcomed the Iranian government's support for Brazil's desire to hold a permanent seat on the Security Council of the United Nations. Some analysts pointed out that Brazil would assume a two-year rotating, non-veto seat in January 2010 and that Iran might hope for Brazilian backing against possible sanctions by the Security Council over its nuclear stance.[41]

The general reaction was one of puzzlement and disappointment. One editorial summarized the mood by pointing out, "Mr. Lula had nothing to say about the bloody suppression of Iran's pro-democracy reform movement."[42] It continued to comment that "Mr. Lula showed why the West would be wise to keep that chair [at the Security Council] on hold."[43] In conclusion, the editorial stated that Brazil must reform its out-of-date and anachronistic third world approach to world affairs.

Once again, some observers argued that the reception of the Iranian head of state was part of the longer-term electoral strategy for 2010 to elect a successor to Lula who will continue his policies. Others argued that it was short-term opportunism, that Brazil had little competence or capacity to resolve a decades-old conflict. Others argued that the trade trump was most important to Brazil over time. Whether any or all of these analyses are relevant, the general impression is that Brasília is in danger of weakening the expectations many countries have of Brazil as an increasingly relevant world player.

Lula, or his successor, will need to understand that an increase in Brazil's profile entails responsible global conduct. If Brazil is to move beyond being considered the permanent "country of tomorrow," it will need to update its diplomacy to match its extraordinary trade and energy potential. Global leaders need to make regional and international decisions that are consistent with overall goals of peace and security. Picking and choosing issues and policies that may have broad domestic appeal for electoral purposes may, over time, be contrary to good foreign policy. All governments wrestle with these complex issues on a daily basis. It remains to be seen, after the 2010 elections in Brazil, whether or not the next administration will grasp that reality.

9 | Conclusion: Brazil Emergent

Brazil's emergence as a player in international affairs is of very recent vintage. As a long-time observer of the country commented recently,

> Continued stability and future growth will require avoiding the mistakes of the past, while finding new solutions to the problems that remain. These include rampant corruption, stalled tax and labor reforms, low levels of domestic saving, inadequate achievements in public education, and not enough highly skilled labor. Successfully resolving such issues would allow Brazil's rise to continue, and Brazil—long viewed as a peripheral country—would finally become a global player.[1]

It is important to place that comment in context. Brazil is half the continent of South America. Its colonial experience was not supportive of national integration given the rapid decline of Portugal in the century following the discovery. While a Brazilian identity emerged by the end of the eighteenth century, it was fragile given the size of the colony and a lack of physical infrastructure to allow for more rapid social and economic integration. Colonial Brazil was a country of "classes and masses." The small white elite presided over a large and marginal population of Afro-Brazilians, forcibly transported from their homeland. Large estates dominated, and the country remained deeply rural well into the nineteenth century.

Education during the colonial era was precarious. Once the Jesuits were expelled in 1759, many of the country's schools basically collapsed. There was no university in Brazil until the Vargas era. Faculties of medicine and law emerged in the late nineteenth and early twentieth centuries, but these were clearly to service the needs of the wealthy bourgeoisie. Social mobility was driven by color and class. With the abolition of slavery in 1888, the former slaves remained beholden to their former masters since they had few other employment options. A new working class appeared in the mid-1880s, composed of immigrants to work on the coffee plantations in the center-south and to make up the first urban service class of storekeepers and small merchants.

While there remains a debate about whether the empire impeded development or did not care, it is clear that there was little entrepreneurship or risk taking in imperial Brazil. The transition to the republic in 1889 was soon dominated by the coffee elites and their allies. A deeply decentralized Brazil saw rampant violence, regional disturbances, and little interest in "Brazilianess" until the 1930s when the new leader of the country, Getúlio Vargas, centralized power in Rio de Janeiro, defeated a separatist movement in São Paulo, and declared a dictatorship in 1937. A middle sector, if not a class, had begun to emerge in the southeastern urban centers around World War I. Vargas quickly co-opted it with a web of public employment, social services, and retirement benefits that opened the door to an ever-growing public sector and expanding public sector debt.

The transition to a democratic state in 1945–46 was once again under the shadow of the armed forces. The two principal presidential candidates in the 1946 national election were military officers. The 1946 republic lasted only eighteen years, and while it saw the beginnings of rapid import substitution industrialization, it was accompanied by erratic fiscal policy, rising inflation, and social and political polarization. The system collapsed in 1964, and the military held power for the next twenty-one years. The regime was peculiar in that it allowed political institutions to function formally, but they were carefully manipulated and purged, as needed. In a masterfully organized civil society movement to restore democratic rule in the early 1980s, the armed forces ceded power, tired and out of answers to the myriad financial and social issues that had not been resolved during their rule.

The 1985 transition was difficult. President-elect Tancredo Neves took ill the day before his inauguration and died soon after. His vice president,

José Sarney, became a truly accidental president. The next nine years witnessed political drift, economic mismanagement, and deepening social problems. It was only with the election of Fernando Henrique Cardoso, following implementation of the *Real* Plan, that there was hope for sustained modernization. Cardoso deserves great credit for his reform efforts, honesty, and sincere commitment to a democratic Brazil. That his government was viewed as only partially successful was due as much to externalities—the financial crises of 1997–99—as to the usual political gridlock in Congress. But without the *Real* Plan and currency, the Lula presidency would have been far less successful.

Lula's eight years provided continuity with the Cardoso presidency. The banking system was modernized and regulated. The export boom during the first years of the new century produced large trade surpluses. The rating agencies finally gave the country an investment-grade rating, which opened many new opportunities for private sector investors. Inflation targeting and the Fiscal Responsibility Law of the Cardoso administration were of great help in reducing debt, balancing the budget, and establishing Brazil as a serious international player. The discovery of massive petroleum and natural gas reserves off the southeast coast created the opportunity for the country to become a major energy player in the next decade. An agricultural giant, Brazil is also the most innovative producer of an increasingly important biofuel: ethanol.

As the Lula administration comes to an end, the question is whether the glass is half full or half empty. This book has attempted to demonstrate that it is the former, for the first time in Brazil's history. Brazil has accomplished what most observers believed to be impossible or highly unlikely. The country of "tomorrow (and always will be)" has become a significant actor today. Political stability is a given. Broadly speaking, Brazil has witnessed the development of two ideological blocs, one center/center-right and one center/center-left. Both are highly participatory, and both follow the rules of the game. While the political process is marred by unseemly levels of corruption, Brazil's electoral system works without glitches, unlike that of many of its neighbors, including the United States. The investigative press is alive, well, and growing. Political contestation is lively, but not polarizing. New actors and players come and go, but all accept the legitimacy of constitutional democracy.

Economically, Brazil has achieved more than stability—it is now a predictable economy. Inflation targeting has buried the historical Achilles' heel of the national economy. With low inflation, individual Brazilians benefit. Combined with the highly successful Bolsa Família program, a new lower middle class of consumers has emerged. Poverty, if not injustice, is being reduced. The trend line is moving in the right direction. Brazil is still too closed an economy, but political leaders understand that, and steps, though not always sufficient, are being taken to further integrate the country into the global economic marketplace. Under President Lula's leadership, Brazil has become the most significant regional actor in South America—a voice for moderation and integration. At the international level, Brazil is now a respected player and interlocutor with both the emerging-market countries and the industrial states. South-South diplomacy has proven to be an effective mechanism for furthering Brazilian political and security interests and for building new diplomatic relations with other emerging actors, especially Russia, India, and China.

There is no doubt that much remains to be done to consolidate and expand Brazil's global role. But it would appear that the progress to date, the subject of this book, and the agenda moving forward ensure that the "crafty superpower" is here to stay. There is every expectation that the third president of Brazil since the turnaround in 1994 will continue with the breakthrough policies of the Cardoso and Lula administrations. His or her inauguration in January 2011 will be one more milestone in the long road to economic and political consolidation, both of which are essential to addressing the continuing challenge of reducing and, it is hoped, eliminating social injustice and poverty. That will be the challenge for the decade ahead, and Brazil appears well prepared to face it.

Notes

Chapter One

1. J. P. Morgan Emerging Markets Research, *Latin America and Caribbean Outlook, 2010* (New York: J. P. Morgan Securities, February 2010), p. 12. All currency amounts in the book are in U.S. dollars unless otherwise stated.

2. Thomas L. Friedman, "A Manifesto for the Fast World," *New York Times Magazine,* March 28, 1999, p. 42.

3. Michael Mandelbaum, *The Ideas That Conquered the World: Peace, Democracy, and Free Markets in the Twenty-first Century* (New York: Public Affairs, 2002).

4. Andrew J. Bacevich, *American Empire: The Realities and Consequences of U.S. Diplomacy* (Harvard University Press, 2002), p. 39.

5. Goldman Sachs, "The World Needs Better Economic BRICs," Economic Research Paper 66 (www2.goldmansachs.com/ideas/brics/building-better-doc.pdf [November 30, 2001]).

6. Bacevich, *American Empire,* p. 39.

7. There are now a number of "Gs"—often confusing—in the world. The original G-6—France, Germany, Italy, Japan, the United Kingdom, and the United States—was created in November 1975. Canada joined the grouping to form the G-7 in 1976, and the European Union is also represented in the group. Russia joined in 1998 to form the G-8; however, G-7 finance ministers and central bank governors have continued to meet without Russia, usually three times a year. Throughout this volume, the grouping is referred to as the G-7, and Russia is considered in the context of the BRIC countries.

8. See Jose Edgardo Campos and Hilton L. Root, *The Key to the Asian Miracle: Making Shared Growth Credible* (Brookings Institution Press, 1996). It is noteworthy that of the eight economies analyzed, neither India nor China was included.

9. Paul Krugman, *The Return of Depression Economics* (New York and London: W. W. Norton, 1999) provides an excellent overview of the origins and implications of the crisis, which involved overvalued and fixed exchange rates, real estate bubbles, faulty central bank data on international reserves, liberalized international capital markets without much regulation, and much more.

10. Edwin M. Truman, *A Strategy for IMF Reform* (Washington: Institute for International Economics, 2006).

11. The Institute for International Economics was at the forefront of the formulation of the Washington consensus. See John Williamson, *The Progress of Policy Reform in Latin America* (Washington: Institute for International Economics, 1990). A more recent publication by Pedro-Pablo Kuczynski and John Williamson, *After the Washington Consensus: Restarting Growth in Latin America* (Washington: Institute for International Economics, 2003), takes stock of what went wrong and what might be done to restart growth and reform.

12. Amy Chua, *World on Fire: How Exporting Free Market Democracy Breeds Ethnic Hatred and Global Instability* (New York and London: Doubleday, 2003); Joseph E. Stiglitz, *Globalization and Its Discontents* (New York and London: W. W. Norton, 2002); Paul Blustein, *The Chastening: Inside the Crisis That Rocked the Global Financial System and Humbled the IMF* (New York: Public Affairs, 2001).

13. Dietmar Rothermund, *India: The Rise of an Asian Giant* (Yale University Press, 2008).

14. David M. Lampton, *The Three Faces of Chinese Power: Might, Money, and Minds* (University of California Press, 2008).

15. Richard Sakwa, *Putin: Russia's Choice* (London and New York: Routledge, 2004).

16. Goldman Sachs, "Dreaming with BRICs: The Path to 2050," Global Economics Paper 99 (www2.goldmansachs.com/ideas/brics/book/99-dreaming.pdf [October 1, 2003]), p. 1. An earlier report, published in 2001, prepared the groundwork for the analysis: Goldman Sachs, "World Needs Better Economic BRICs."

17. Goldman Sachs, "Dreaming with BRICs"; Goldman Sachs, "World Needs Better Economic BRICs."

18. Goldman Sachs, "How Solid Are the BRICs?" Global Economics Paper 134 (www2.goldmansachs.com/ideas/brics/how-solid-doc.pdf [December 1, 2005]), p. 3.

19. Goldman Sachs, "How Solid Are the BRICs?"

20. Goldman Sachs, "How Solid Are the BRICs?"

21. Goldman Sachs, "How Solid Are the BRICs?"

22. This is the Trade G-20 (as opposed to the Financial G-20). The Trade G-20's principal goal is to foster negotiations in agriculture, and the group has continually fought for lower U.S. agricultural subsidies. The group consists of twenty-three member countries, representing 60 percent of the world population and 26 percent of the world's agricultural exports; it is led by Brazil, China, India, and South Africa.

23. James Lamont, "India Damps Hope of Reviving Doha Talks," *Financial Times,* July 30, 2009, p. 3. The article reports the Indian commerce secretary as stating that any agreement was out of reach while the world's political leaders faced public anger in their countries over job losses and lack of economic growth.

24. Peter Baker, "Poorer Nations Reject a Target on Emission Cut," *New York Times,* July 9, 2009, p. A1.

25. George Parker and Guy Dinmore, "Arguments over How Many to Invite to the Party," *Financial Times,* July 11–12, 2009, p. 2.

26. David Oakley and Patti Waldmeir, "Developing Nations Shine amid the Crisis Gloom," *Financial Times,* July 28, 2009, p. 19.

27. The Financial G-20 was established in September 1999 in the aftermath of the 1997 Asian financial crisis and designed to bring together industrial and developing countries to discuss key issues facing the global economy. It met for the first time in Berlin in December 1999 and since then has met annually at the level of finance ministers or central bank governors. The November 2008 Washington summit was the first G-20 meeting to take place at the level of heads of state or government. The Financial G-20 membership represents 90 percent of global GNP and 67 percent of the world's population and is composed of Argentina, Australia, Brazil, Canada, China, France, Germany, India, Indonesia, Italy, Japan, Mexico, Russia, Saudi Arabia, South Africa, South Korea, Turkey, the United Kingdom, the United States, and the European Union. The European Central Bank attends as an "institutional" member, along with the IMF and the World Bank. The nineteen countries (the EU being the twentieth member) in the G-20 are not the world's largest economies, and the London summit was attended by a larger group than the G-20. Three countries are members of the G-20 but outside of the top twenty economies: South Africa, Saudi Arabia, and Argentina.

28. Finance ministers of the four BRIC countries had met in São Paulo, Brazil, days before the Washington summit. The ministers "called for the reform of multilateral institutions in order that they reflect the structural changes in the world economy and the increasingly central role that emerging markets now play." See "Emerging Powers Join Forces for Finance Reform," Thomson Reuters, November 7, 2008.

29. G-20, "Declaration: Summit on Financial Markets and the World Economy" (Washington: G-20, November 15, 2008).

30. G-20, "The Global Plan for Recovery and Reform" (Washington: G-20, April 2, 2009).

31. Edmund L. Andrews, "Leaders of G-20 Vow to Reshape Global Economy," *New York Times,* September 25, 2009.

32. Andrews, "Leaders of G-20 Vow to Reshape."

33. "Key Accomplishments of the Group of 20 Pittsburgh Summit" (White House, Office of the Press Secretary, September 25, 2009).

34. "Leaders' Statement: The Pittsburgh Summit" (www.pittsburghsummit.gov [September 24–25, 2009]).

35. "Another BRIC in the Wall," *The Economist,* April 21, 2008. John Browne, "BRIC Threat to U.S. Dollar Reserve Currency," *Asia Sentinel,* June 18, 2009.

36. The excess dollars fill up in foreign central banks, leaving those countries with a difficult choice: reinvest the dollars in U.S. securities or hold them and face an increase in the value of their own currencies, making their products less competitive in world markets.

37. Liz Rappaport and James T. Areddy, "Bond Worry: Will China Keep Buying?" *Wall Street Journal,* July 31, 2009, p. C2.

38. David Barboza, "China Urges New Money Reserve to Replace Dollar," *New York Times,* March 23, 2009.

39. Clifford J. Levy, "Seeking Greater Financial Clout, Emerging Powers Prepare to Meet in Russia," *New York Times,* June 16, 2009, p. A6.

40. Andrew Osborn, "Four Developing Powers Seek Global Clout," *Wall Street Journal,* June 17, 2009, p. A6.

41. "A BRIC in the Wall," *Financial Times,* editorial, June 10, 2009.

42. "A BRIC in the Wall." Mr. O'Neill is the Goldman Sachs Group's head of global economic research and leader of the team that coined the term BRICs in 2001.

43. See Michael Orme, "BRIC Star Brazil," *Daily Reckoning* (www.daily reckoning.co.uk/emerging-market-investment/bric-star-brazil.html [October 17, 2007]).

Chapter Two

1. See Boris Fausto, *A Concise History of Brazil* (Cambridge University Press, 1999); E. Bradford Burns, *A History of Brazil,* 2d ed. (Columbia University Press, 1980); Peter Flynn, *Brazil: A Political Analysis* (Boulder, Colo.: Westview Press, 1978).

2. In the Portuguese empire, captaincies referred to the administrative divisions and hereditary fiefs that divided the colonies. Initially, Brazil comprised fifteen hereditary captaincies. With the increased importance of Brazil as a Portuguese colony, and in an effort to centralize the colony, the captaincies became two viceroyalties—Brazil and Grão Pará in 1763—and were finally united under the viceroyalty of Brazil in 1775.

3. Celso Furtado, *The Economic Growth of Brazil: A Survey from Colonial to Modern Times* (University of California Press, 1963).

4. Caio Prado Jr., *The Colonial Background of Modern Brazil* (University of California Press, 1967).

5. Gilberto Freyre, *The Masters and the Slaves: A Study in the Development of Brazilian Civilization* (New York: Alfred A. Knopf, 1970).

6. Anthony W. Marx, *Making Race and Nation: A Comparison of the United States, South Africa, and Brazil* (Cambridge University Press, 1998), p. 50.

7. Leslie Bethell, *Brazil: Empire and Republic, 1822–1930* (Cambridge University Press, 1989).

8. In 1822 only a small portion of literate men were given the right to vote; women, non-Catholics, and people with modest incomes were excluded. The 1881 Saraiva Law allowed non-Catholics, freedmen, and naturalized citizens to vote, but instituted two new requirements: literacy and proof of income. James Holston,

Insurgent Citizenship: Disjunctions of Democracy and Modernity in Brazil (Princeton University Press, 2008), p. 101.

9. Werner Baer, *The Brazilian Economy: Growth and Development*, 6th ed. (Boulder, Colo.: Lynne Rienner, 2008), p. 19.

10. Thomas E. Skidmore, *Black into White: Race and Nationality in Brazilian Thought* (Oxford University Press, 1974).

11. For a sympathetic overview of the role of the emperor, see Roderick J. Barman, *Citizen Emperor: Pedro II and the Making of Brazil, 1825–91* (Stanford University Press, 1999).

12. For a devastating analysis of the debate in Brazil over the country's future, see Euclides da Cunha, *Rebellion in the Backlands* (University of Chicago Press, 1944).

13. Baer, *Brazilian Economy*, p. 34.

Chapter Three

1. Thomas E. Skidmore, *Politics in Brazil, 1930–1964: An Experiment in Democracy* (Oxford University Press, 1967), p. 40.

2. For a sensitive analysis of the emergence of the middle class in Brazil, see Brian P. Owensby, *Intimate Ironies: Modernity and the Making of Middle-Class Lives in Brazil* (Stanford University Press, 1999).

3. Bradford Burns, *A History of Brazil* (Columbia University Press, 1970).

4. Burns, *History of Brazil*, p. 302.

5. Lincoln Gordon, *Brazil's Second Chance: En Route toward the First World* (Brookings Institution Press, 2001), p. 14.

6. Gordon, *Brazil's Second Chance*.

7. For more information on the National Student Union, visit www.une.org.br.

8. Skidmore, *Politics in Brazil*, p. 52.

9. The 1824 constitution that survived until the end of the empire in 1889 gave the emperor the power to dissolve the Chamber of Deputies and to call for new elections, to approve or veto decisions of both the Chamber of Deputies and the Senate, and to moderate disputes. At the end of the empire, it was generally assumed that the army had assumed the moderating power (*poder moderador*) of the emperor to change governments when the armed forces determined it was in the best interest of the nation.

10. Skidmore, *Politics in Brazil*.

11. By the mid-1940s Brazil was still heavily dependent on one commodity—coffee—for its foreign exchange earnings.

12. The debate over the appropriate role of the state would remain controversial until the 1990s, when the *Real* Plan was implemented and began the process of taking the state out of the economy. In this period, those who favored a smaller role for the state in the economy were often referred to as *entreguistas*.

13. Gordon, *Brazil's Second Chance*, p. 16.

14. For background on this period, see Riordan Roett, *The Politics of Foreign Aid in the Brazilian Northeast* (Vanderbilt University Press, 1972).

15. For an in-depth analysis of this phenomenon, see Emanuel de Kadt, *Catholic Radicals in Brazil* (Oxford University Press, 1970).

16. For more on this, see Skidmore, *Politics in Brazil*, pp. 194–200.

17. During the first Vargas regime in the 1930s, many reforms were introduced to favor the emerging middle class through government jobs, social security, and retirement benefits. Following his return to power in 1951, Vargas shifted course and favored the working class and the poor, to the dismay of the middle class.

18. Skidmore, *Politics in Brazil*, p. 262.

19. Svengali was a character in a nineteenth-century novel that manipulates or exerts excessive control over another.

20. Alfred Stepan, *The Military in Politics: Changing Patterns in Brazil* (Princeton University Press, 1971).

Chapter Four

1. Thomas E. Skidmore, *Black into White: Race and Nationality in Brazilian Thought* (Oxford University Press, 1974), p. 308.

2. Werner Baer, *The Brazilian Economy: Growth and Development*, 6th ed. (Boulder, Colo.: Lynne Rienner, 2008), p. 75.

3. There had been an early warning that the opposition was still popular when, in the São Paulo mayoral elections in March, a candidate endorsed by former president Jânio Quadros defeated the government candidate.

4. So-called because of their training in the orthodox Economics Department at the University of Chicago in the 1960s.

5. Lincoln Gordon, *Brazil's Second Chance: En Route toward the First World* (Brookings Institution Press, 2001), p. 21.

6. Baer, *Brazilian Economy*, p. 87.

7. The fifth institutional act stated that the "revolutionary process unfolding could not be detained." This act permitted the president to recess the national Congress, state legislative assemblies, and municipal councils by complementary acts. These bodies would only reconvene when called by the president. The president could also declare an intervention of the state if perceived to be in the national interest, without regard for the constitution or political rights. Riordan Roett, *Brazil: Politics in a Patrimonial Society*, 5th ed. (Westport, Conn.: Praeger, 1999), pp. 26, 136.

8. Roett, *Brazil*, p. 63.

9. Alfred Stepan, *The Military in Politics: Changing Patterns in Brazil* (Princeton University Press, 1971), pp. 253–66.

10. Stepan, *Military in Politics*, p. 254.

11. The April package instituted an indirect selection process for one senator from each state. Each state was assigned three senators, two elected directly and one indirectly (known as "bionic" senators), all of whom would hold office for eight years. This reform package also retained the indirect electoral college system to elect the president and state governors.

12. Limitations had been put in place to reduce the president's power to close Congress, and participation of political parties was expanded. See Roett, *Brazil*, p. 150.

13. In 1911 a Register of Similar Products was established. The Law of Similars allowed Brazilian producers to gain tariff protection from imported goods by placing a heavy tariff on imported products similar to those being produced within Brazil. See Baer, *Brazilian Economy,* p. 58. The deposit requirements on capital inflows refer to the proportion of funds borrowed from abroad that a bank must hold in reserves with the central bank.

14. See Roett, *Brazil,* p. 148.

Chapter Five

1. International Monetary Fund, International Financial Statistics, Brazil, 1984 (www.imfstatistics.org).

2. Werner Baer, *The Brazilian Economy: Growth and Development,* 6th ed. (Boulder, Colo.: Lynne Rienner, 2008), p. 99.

3. Lincoln Gordon, *Brazil's Second Chance: En Route toward the First World* (Brookings Institution Press, 2001), p. 3.

4. The law called for automatic semiannual readjustments of wages of 110 percent of the inflation rate for low-income workers.

5. Lourdes Sola, "Heterodox Shock in Brazil: *Técnicos,* Politicians, and Democracy," *Journal of Latin American Studies* 23, no. 1 (February 1991): 163–95.

6. Thomas E. Skidmore, *The Politics of Military Rule in Brazil, 1964–85* (Oxford University Press, 1988), p. 278.

7. Baer, *Brazilian Economy,* pp. 110–19.

8. For a personal analysis of the origins of the *Real* Plan, see Fernando Henrique Cardoso, *The Accidental President of Brazil: A Memoir* (New York: Public Affairs, 2006), ch. 9.

9. Cardoso, *Accidental President,* p. 75.

10. Cardoso, *Accidental President,* p. 133, original source: *Boletin Conjuntural,* October 1996.

11. Cardoso, *Accidental President.*

12. Cardoso, *Accidental President.*

13. Cardoso, *Accidental President,* original source: *Exame,* June 5, 1995, p. 27.

Chapter Six

1. In 1994–98, while federal state-owned enterprises had a surplus amounting to 0.4 percent of GDP, state and municipal state-owned enterprises had a surplus amounting to 0.7 percent of GDP. Werner Baer, *The Brazilian Economy: Growth and Development,* 6th ed. (Boulder, Colo.: Lynne Rienner, 2008), p. 231.

2. For more information regarding privatization, see Baer, *Brazilian Economy,* ch. 10.

3. For decades, beginning with the Vargas regime in the 1930s, public sector employment had been used to build political support. The jobs carried a lifetime guarantee, with very generous benefits such as retirement payments. Over the years, it became impossible to reduce those benefits, and the social security costs skyrocketed.

4. Baer, *Brazilian Economy,* p. 130.

5. Baer, *Brazilian Economy,* p. 137.

6. For an overview of the crisis, see Riordan Roett, ed., *The Mexican Peso Crisis: International Perspectives* (Boulder, Colo.: Lynne Rienner, 1996).

7. Celso L. Martone, "Recent Economic Policy in Brazil before and after the Mexican Peso Crisis," in *The Mexican Peso Crisis,* edited by Roett, p. 61.

8. Lincoln Gordon, *Brazil's Second Chance: En Route toward the First World* (Brookings Institution Press, 2001), p. 187.

9. Gordon, *Brazil's Second Chance,* p. 188.

10. Peter Isard, *Globalization and the International Financial System: What's Wrong and What Can Be Done?* (Cambridge University Press, 2005), pp. 148–49.

11. Gordon, *Brazil's Second Chance,* p. 189.

12. Long-Term Capital Management was a U.S. hedge fund that used trading strategies such as fixed-income arbitrage, statistical arbitrage, and pairs trading, combined with high leverage. Its failure resulted in a massive bailout by other major banks and investment houses, under pressure from the Federal Reserve. Enormously successful in its first years, in 1998 it lost $4.6 billion in less than four months. The fund closed in early 2000.

13. International Monetary Fund, *The IMF and Recent Capital Account Crises: Indonesia, Korea, and Brazil* (Washington: IMF, 2003), p. 22.

14. Baer, *Brazilian Economy,* p. 146.

15. Baer, *Brazilian Economy.*

16. See Edmund Amann and Werner Baer, "The Illusion of Stability: The Brazilian Economy under Cardoso," *World Development* 28, no. 10 (October 2000): 1805–19.

17. Amann and Baer, "Illusion of Stability."

18. International Monetary Fund, *The IMF and Recent Capital Account Crises,* p. 131.

19. Peter Flynn, "Brazil: The Politics of Crisis," *Third World Quarterly* 20, no. 2 (April 1999): 290.

20. Gordon, *Brazil's Second Chance,* p. 191.

21. Frederic Mishkin, "Inflation Targeting in Emerging-Market Countries," *American Economic Review* 90, no. 2 (May 2003): 105.

22. Pedro-Pablo Kuczynski and John Williamson, eds., *After the Washington Consensus: Restating Growth and Reform in Latin America* (Washington: Institute for International Economics, 2003); Sebastian Edwards, "Forty Years of Latin America's Economic Development: From the Alliance for Progress to the Washington Consensus," NBER Working Paper 15190 (Cambridge, Mass.: National Bureau of Economic Research, July 2009), p. 28.

23. Kuczynski and Williamson, *After the Washington Consensus;* Edwards, "Forty Years."

24. Peter Kingstone and Timothy Power, eds., *Democratic Brazil Revisited* (University of Pittsburgh Press, 2008), p. 137.

25. Broadly, political risk refers to the complications that businesses and governments may face as a result of what are commonly referred to as political decisions—or any political change that alters the expected outcome and value

of a given economic action by changing the probability of achieving business objectives.

26. Political Database of the Americas, "Brazil: 2002 Presidential Election/ Eleições Presidenciais de 2002" (Georgetown University and the Organization of American States, 2005), pdba.georgetown.edu/Elecdata/Brazil/pres02.html.

27. Antônio Palocci is a medical doctor and a founding member of the PT in São Paulo. He served as a councilman and mayor of his home town, Ribeirão Preto, resigning to join Lula's 2002 presidential campaign.

28. Anthony W. Marx, *Making Race and Nation: A Comparison of the United States, South Africa, and Brazil* (Cambridge University Press, 1998).

29. For the origins of the cash transfer programs in Brazil, see Marcus Andre Melo, "Unexpected Successes, Unanticipated Failures," in *Democratic Brazil Revisited*, edited by Kingstone and Power, ch. 8.

30. In writing the foreword to President Cardoso's memoir, former U.S. president Bill Clinton commented, "[Cardoso] assumed the presidency of a young democracy with an unstable economy, and he transformed Brazil into a mature and prosperous nation respected around the world." Fernando Enrique Cardoso, *The Accidental President of Brazil: A Memoir* (New York: Public Affairs, 2006), p. xi.

31. Aline Diniz Amaral, Peter R. Kingstone, and Jonathan Krieckhaus, "The Limits of Economic Reform in Brazil," in *Democratic Brazil Revisited*, edited by Kingstone and Power, p. 142.

Chapter Seven

1. Goldman Sachs, "How Solid Are the BRICs?" Global Economics Paper 134 (www2.goldmansachs.com/ideas/brics/how-solid-doc.pdf [December 1, 2005]), p. 1.

2. John Williamson, "Is Brazil Next?" Policy Brief 02-7 (Washington: Institute for International Economics), p. 5.

3. *Financial Times*, October 23, 2002, p. 19.

4. Timothy J. Power, "Centering Democracy? Ideological Cleavages and Convergence in the Brazilian Political Class," in *Democratic Brazil Revisited*, edited by Peter Kingstone and Timothy Power (University of Pittsburgh Press, 2008), p. 82.

5. Werner Baer, *The Brazilian Economy: Growth and Development*, 6th ed. (Boulder, Colo.: Lynne Rienner, 2008), p. 156.

6. Goldman Sachs, "Dreaming with BRICs: The Path to 2050," Global Economics Paper 99 (www2.goldmansachs.com/ideas/brics/book/99-dreaming.pdf [October 1, 2003]), p. 10.

7. Goldman Sachs, "Dreaming with BRICs," p. 15.

8. Baer, *Brazilian Economy*, p. 166.

9. Baer, *Brazilian Economy*, p. 164.

10. Wendy Hunter and Natasha Borges Sugiyama, "Democracy and Social Policy in Brazil: Advancing Basic Needs, Preserving Privileged Interests," *Latin American Politics and Society* 51, no. 2 (Summer 2009): 46.

11. For more on this, see Kathy Lindert, "Brazil: Bolsa Família Program— Scaling up Cash Transfers to the Poor," in *MfDR Principles in Action: Sourcebook*

on Emerging Good Practices, 1st ed. (Paris: OECD; Washington: World Bank, 2006), pp. 67–74. Available at www.oecd.org/dataoecd/35/10/36853468.pdf.

12. Hunter and Sugiyama, "Democracy and Social Policy," p. 47.

13. Janice Perlman, "Redemocratization Viewed from Below: Urban Poverty and Politics in Rio de Janeiro, 1968–2005," in *Democratic Brazil Revisited,* edited by Kingstone and Power, p. 278.

14. Historically, there was little interest in educating the poor and marginal sectors of the population. Well into the twentieth century, education was for the middle and upper classes. While there were public schools, they were generally of poor quality, and, as a consequence, a parallel system of private education evolved. Those supporting the private school system had little interest in the quality of public schools.

15. "Brazil's Poor Schools: Still a Lot to Learn," *The Economist,* June 6, 2009, pp. 36–37.

16. Baer, *Brazilian Economy,* p. 156.

17. For further reading on the changes in Lula's voter base, see Wendy Hunter and Timothy J. Power, "Rewarding Lula: Executive Power, Social Policy, and the Brazilian Elections of 2006," *Latin American Politics and Society* 49, no. 1 (Spring 2007): 1–30.

18. Hunter and Power, "Rewarding Lula," p. 1.

19. Hunter and Power, "Rewarding Lula," p. 4.

20. See www.standardandpoors.com/ratingsdirect (April 30, 2008).

21. Hunter and Power, "Rewarding Lula," p. 2.

22. See "Sovereigns Brazil Credit Analysis" (www.fitchratings.com).

23. "UPDATE 1-Petrobras Confirms Potential Tupi Oil Reserves," *Reuters.com,* November 12, 2009.

24. "Brazil to Open up Vast Offshore Fields," *Financial Times,* May 29, 2009, p. 6. The announcement that Brazil is preparing a new round of bidding for concessions in the "pre-salt" fields as early as 2010 was welcomed by the major international oil companies, which have become disillusioned with prospects in Mexico and Venezuela, where political interference by the government has made it almost impossible to operate.

25. A recent study reports that Petrobras entered the biofuels domain after much resistance. But the target of expanding the company's participation in the ethanol market is part of its 2007–11 business plan. To secure the increase in supply, partnerships are being studied in more than forty alcohol production projects. Petrobras exported 80 million liters of alcohol in 2006 and is planning to multiply its sales abroad. To this end, the company will invest more than $1.6 billion in ethanol production, storage, transportation, and distribution. In addition, the state-owned firm is implementing its first industrial biofuel production units, which will generate 171 million liters of alcohol a year. See Ricardo Ubiraci Sennes and Thais Narciso, "Brazil as an International Energy Player," in *Brazil as an Economic Superpower? Understanding Brazil's Changing Role in the Global Economy,* edited by Lael Brainard and Leonardo Martínez-Diaz (Brookings Institution Press, 2009), p. 39.

26. "Biofuels: The Promises and the Risks," in *World Development Report 2008* (Washington: World Bank, 2008). Also see Daniel Budny and Paulo

Sotero, eds., *Brazil Institute Special Report: The Global Dynamics of Biofuels* (Washington: Brazil Institute, Woodrow Wilson Center, 2008).

27. These three are Itaú Unibanco (number five with a market capitalization of $92.3 billion), Bradesco (number seven with $60.1 billion), and Banco do Brasil (number nine with $43.6 billion). Patrick Jenkins, "China Banks Eclipse U.S. Rivals," *Financial Times*, January 10, 2010.

28. Quote from Alvise Marino of IDEAglobal; taken from Jonathan Wheatley, "Investing in Brazil," *Financial Times*, November 5, 2009.

29. Central Bank of Brazil, Economic Indicators, Foreign Financial System Credit Operations (www.bcb.gov.br/?english).

30. Lynn Cowan and Rogerio Jelmayer, "Year's Biggest IPOs Make Debuts," *Wall Street Journal*, October 8, 2009.

31. "The Top 40 Sustainable Banks," *Latin Finance*, September 1, 2009.

32. As defined by Geert Bekaert, Campbell R. Harvey, and Christian T. Lundblad, "Equity Market Liberalization in Emerging Markets," *Federal Reserve Bank of St. Louis Report* 85, no. 4 (2003): 54.

33. Barbara Stallings, *Finance for Development* (Brookings Institution Press, 2006), p. 230.

34. An ADR represents ownership in the shares of a non-U.S. company and trades in U.S. financial markets.

35. Bekaert, Harvey, and Lundbland, "Equity Market Liberalization," p. 56.

36. Stallings, *Finance for Development*, p. 248.

37. A global depository receipt is a receipt for shares in a foreign-based corporation traded in capital markets around the world.

38. Economist Intelligence Unit, "Brazil Country Finance" (London: EIU, 2009).

39. International Monetary Fund, "Global Financial Stability Report: Navigating the Financial Challenges Ahead," Washington, D.C., October 2009, p. 219 (Table 24, "Bank Nonperforming Loans to Total Loans").

40. Lionel Barber and Jonathan Wheatley, "Brazil Keeps Its Economic Excitement in Check," *Financial Times*, October 26, 2009, p. 4.

Chapter Eight

1. "Getting It Together at Last: A Special Report on Business and Finance in Brazil," *The Economist*, November 14, 2009; Lionel Barber and Jonathan Wheatley, "The Real Reward," *Financial Times*, November 9, 2009, p. 7.

2. Indeed, in rejecting the FTAA, President Chávez has overseen the formation of the Alternativa Bolivariana para las Américas (the Bolivarian Alternative for the Americas). Based on the EU model, Chávez wants the emphasis of his organization to be on energy and infrastructure agreements that will be extended gradually to other priority development objectives of all of the countries in the Americas.

3. "South American Block Born: Twelve Countries Join Together in the South American Community," Inter-Press Service, December 23, 2004.

4. Since its founding, the Rio Group has proven to be an efficient mechanism for permanent consultation with the European Union. The first ministerial meeting

between the EU and the Rio Group was in 1990. Since then, foreign ministers of the two regions have met every two years, alternating with the years of the summits between the EU and Latin America and the Caribbean. Dialogue between the two entities also takes place regularly at the United Nations General Assembly to discuss issues related to multilateralism and the international agenda. The EU foreign ministers met with their counterparts from the Rio Group in May 2009 in Prague (Czech Republic) to discuss issues of major concern to both regions, notably the impact of the economic and financial crisis and a sustainable approach to energy security and climate change.

5. For an earlier, optimistic view of Mercosur, see Riordan Roett, ed., *Mercosur: Regional Integration, World Markets* (Boulder, Colo.: Lynne Rienner, 1999).

6. It is arguable that Mercosur is much more useful to Brazil as a political instrument in its relations in the Southern Cone. The economy of Brazil so dominates the subregion that Brazil, as a global player, does not need the economic cooperation of the members. But in terms of a political alliance, it is very useful to Brasília to use the common market mechanism to "keep an eye" on the neighbors, especially Argentina. While bilateral relations are normal, there is an abiding jealousy in Buenos Aires that the "upstart" country, Brazil, is now the dominant player in the region. Argentina's constant series of economic and political crises contrast sharply with the consolidation of institutions in Brazil.

7. MINUSTAH was established on June 1, 2004. Brookings Institution and the Woodrow Wilson Center, *New Directions in Brazilian Foreign Relations* (Washington: Brookings/Woodrow Wilson Center, 2007).

8. See "IBSA: An International Actor and Partner for the EU?" Working Paper 63 (Madrid: Fundación para Las Relaciones Internacionales y El Diálogo Exterior, July 2008). See also Woodrow Wilson International Center for Scholars, "Emerging Powers: India, Brazil, and South Africa (IBSA) and the Future of South-South Cooperation," Special Report (Washington: Woodrow Wilson Center, August 2009).

9. "IBSA: An International Actor," p. 4.

10. "Russia and Brazil Heads Push Ties," *BBC News,* November 28, 2008 (news.bbc.co.uk/2/hi/7750837.stm).

11. Paulo Sotero quoted in "Latin American Diplomacy: Friends of Opportunity," *The Economist,* November 27, 2008.

12. "Brazil and China Forge Closer Trade Links," *BBC News,* May 19, 2009 (news.bbc.co.uk/2/hi/business/8057048.stm).

13. President Lula and China's president first discussed the idea at the April 2009 London summit. Jonathan Wheatley, "Brazil and China in Plan to Axe Dollar," *Financial Times,* May 19, 2009, p. 6. The governor of the Chinese central bank, Zhou Xiaochuan, earlier this year proposed replacing the U.S. dollar as the world's leading currency with a new international reserve currency, possibly in the form of special drawing rights used by the International Monetary Fund.

14. "Russian Agriculture Minister Hails Ties with BRIC Countries," *BBC Worldwide Monitoring,* March 26, 2010.

15. See Lael Brainard and Leonardo Martínez-Diaz, eds., *Brazil as an Economic Superpower? Understanding Brazil's Changing Role in the Global Economy* (Brookings Institution Press, 2009).

16. The Singapore issues were the result of the first WTO ministerial conference held in Singapore in 1996. The meeting established permanent working groups on four issues: transparency in government procurement, trade facilitation (customs issues), trade and investment, and trade and competition. These issues were discussed at successive ministerial meetings by the European Union, the United States, Japan, and South Korea. The developing countries opposed them. Since no compromise agreement appeared possible, the developed nations insisted that any new trade negotiations must include these issues.

17. Brazil, for example, would have accepted a 56 percent cut in its industrial tariffs.

18. John W. Miller, "Global Trade Talks Fail as New Giants Flex Muscle," *Wall Street Journal*, July 3, 2008, p. 1.

19. Andrew Batson, "China Casts Its Lot with Developing Nations," *Wall Street Journal*, July 31, 2008.

20. www.g20.org/about_faq.aspx.

21. G-7 members are the United States, France, Germany, Italy, Japan, the United Kingdom, and Canada.

22. "Brazil Pushes for Bigger G-20 Role," *BBC News*, March 26, 2009 (news.bbc.co.uk/2/hi/business/7963704.stm).

23. See www.expressbuzz.com/edition/print.aspx?artid=D1VQXo68m14.

24. See www.expressbuzz.com/edition/print.aspx?artid=D1VQXo68m14.

25. The Financial Stability Forum was founded in 1999 to promote international financial stability. The original membership included about a dozen nations, which participated through their central banks, financial ministries, and securities regulators. At the 2009 G-20 summit, it was decided to establish a successor called the Financial Stability Board, which would include those members of the G-20 that were not members of the Financial Stability Forum.

26. G-20, *Declaration: Summit of Financial Markets and the World Economy* (Washington: G-20, November 15, 2008).

27. Ministry of Finance of the Russian Federation, "BRIC Finance Ministers' Communiqué" (Horsham, U.K., March 13, 2009). www1.minfin.ru/en/index.php?pg56=3&id56=7173.

28. Ministry of Finance of the Russian Federation, "BRIC Finance Ministers' Communiqué."

29. G-20, *The Global Plan for Recovery and Reform* (Washington: G-20, April 2, 2009).

30. "Lula Blames Rich Nations for Crisis," *AlJazeera English*, September 30, 2008.

31. " 'Blue-Eyed Bankers' to Blame for Crash, Lula Tells Brown," *Guardian*, March 26, 2009 (www.guardian.co.uk/world/2009/mar/26/lula-attacks-white-bankers-crash).

32. "EU Holds First Summit in Brazil" (europa.eu/rapid/pressReleasesAction.do?reference=IP/07/1001&format=HTML&age [July 3, 2007]).

33. "France Backs Brazil's UN Ambition," *BBC News,* December 23, 2008 (news.bbc.co.uk/2/hi/europe/7796776.stm).

34. Brookings and Woodrow Wilson Center, *New Directions.*

35. "Brazil's Foreign Policy: Lula and His Squabbling Friends," *The Economist,* August 13, 2009.

36. "Latin American Leaders Aim to Redefine Relationship with United States," *New York Times,* April 17, 2009.

37. Mac Margolis, "The Crafty Superpower," *Newsweek,* April 27, 2009.

38. Barber and Wheatley, "The Real Reward," p. 7.

39. "Getting It Together at Last," p. 16.

40. "Getting It Together at Last."

41. In late November 2009 the International Atomic Energy Agency issued a rebuke to Iran for secretly building a second enrichment plant. Brazil, along with five other countries, abstained from voting. The resolution by the thirty-five-member Board of Governors called on Iran to halt uranium enrichment and immediately freeze the construction of its Fordo nuclear facility, located near Qom. The Brazilian delegate explained the abstention by stating that the resolution clears the way for sanctions, and sanctions will only result in a hardening of the Iranian position.

42. "A Hug from Lula," *Washington Post,* November 26, 2009.

43. "A Hug from Lula."

Chapter Nine

1. Juan de Onis, "Brazil's Big Moment," *Foreign Affairs* 87, no. 6 (November–December 2008): 111.

Index